SOCCER
FOR THE FIRST-TIME COACH

Butch Lauffer & Sandy Davie

Sterling Publishing Co., Inc.
New York

Dedication

To my lovely wife Kimberly, who I love more than she will ever know and who has kept our family together, my two children, Kendall and Kyle, who have given me so much pleasure and love that any proud father could ask for, and my parents Bob and Ann, who I think of everyday as I try to live my life based on the values they taught me.
—Butch Lauffer

To my loving wife Suzanne, without whose love and support I would not have achieved half as much as I have. Also, to the countless numbers of people who influenced my playing and coaching career, I thank you.—Sandy Davie

Photographer: Steven Line
Artist: Rob Carboni
Fitness Consultant: Eric Davis
Athletic Trainer: Michael Landis
Players for photos: Drifters Soccer Club
Book Design: Vicky Vaughn
Editor: Rodman P. Neumann

Library of Congress Cataloging-in-Publication Data
Lauffer, Robert.
  Soccer for the first-time coach / Butch Lauffer & Sandy Davie.
     p. cm.
  Rev. ed. of: Soccer coach's guide to practices, drills & skill training, ©1991.
  Includes index.
  ISBN 1-4027-2598-1
  1. Soccer—Coaching. 2. Soccer—Training. I. Davie, Sandy. II. Title.

GV943.8.L39 2006
796.334'07'7—dc22

2005024124

10 9 8 7 6 5 4 3 2 1

Published by Sterling Publishing Co., Inc.
387 Park Avenue South, New York, NY 10016
© 2006 by Robert "Butch" Lauffer & Alexander "Sandy" Davie
Revised edition of: *Soccer Coach's Guide to Practices, Drills & Skill Training,* © 1991.
Distributed in Canada by Sterling Publishing
c/o Canadian Manda Group, 165 Dufferin Street
Toronto, Ontario, Canada M6K 3H6
Distributed in the United Kingdom by GMC Distribution
Services, Castle Place, 166 High Street, Lewes,
East Sussex, England BN7 1XU
Distributed in Australia by Capricorn Link (Australia) Pty. Ltd.
P.O. Box 704, Windsor, NSW 2756, Australia

Printed in China
All rights reserved

Sterling ISBN-13: 978-1-4027-2598-2
          ISBN-10: 1-4027-2598-1

For information about custom editions, special sales, premium andcorporate purchases, please contact Sterling Special Sales Department at 800-805-5489 or specialsales@sterlingpub.com.

Contents

Acknowledgments

I tell my players all the time that life and the game of soccer are about decisions and choices. The players and team who makes the most correct decisions and choices usually win the game. For me, the decision to ask Kimberly K. Gilbert to marry me and the choice she made to accept my proposal allows me now to look back and see how lucky I am. She has continually shown her patience and love with all my soccer travels and endeavors. I want my daughter Kendall to always remember how intelligent she is and that she can achieve anything she desires. And my son Kyle has grown into a young boy who is intellectual and has such an enthusiasm for life.

I also want to acknowledge my co-author, Sandy Davie, and his lovely wife Sue. Thank you from the bottom of my heart for being such great friends. Kim and I both wish New Zealand were closer and maybe I will finally figure out the time difference.

I must thank West Texas A&M University, the Athletic Department, and all of the assistant coaches and players who have passed through our program. In the Athletic Department I especially want to thank Holly Troth, Mike Chandler, and Ed Harris. Also a thank you goes to all the other athletic staff, past and present; you have allowed me the opportunity to grow professionally and develop my craft.

And I want to thank the game, itself, that has allowed me to have so many great experiences around the world by letting me be an ambassador of the sport. I hope it never stops.

—Butch Lauffer

Introduction

Since its inception, the fine art of soccer has captivated people's passion and imagination from all around the globe. As the game's popularity has continued to grow, there has been an ever-increasing need for more parent and volunteer coaches at the grassroots level.

This book has been specifically designed to aid the parent or volunteer coach, by providing a framework around which a proper training program of instruction can be created. There are problems that can affect the inexperienced youth soccer coach. With some thought these can be avoided.

The first and second chapters contain basic reference material—on techniques and skills development from dribbling to goalkeeping on the one hand, to injury prevention and team management on the other.

To further ease the learning process, the remaining four chapters represent a tool for the novice coach to choose, plan, and create a practicing strategy that will accomplish the goals of technique mastery and team development while encouraging the players' sense of fun and enjoyment. These four chapters cover the four young age-groups—Under 8, Under 10, Under 12, and Under 15—outlining player and goalkeeping practices along with team games. Each of these practices can be expanded upon as the players progress. We encourage the coach to think of new ways to adapt the exercises and to use them as inspiration for designing original practices suited to a particular need.

In addition to helping the coach develop the player's skills and techniques, the object of this book is to encourage the player's sense of enjoyment. It must be emphasized that youth soccer should be about the players and not an opportunity for coaches, or parents, to live out their own hopes and aspirations through their children. Never delude yourself: You are not the head coach of your favorite college team or your country's national team. Youth soccer is not the place to prove to the world that you are a tactical genius. Your job is to ensure that your players enjoy playing the game.

Remember that it is a child that you are working with. Avoid complicated instructions and take into consideration the players' capacity to understand those instructions. Explain the purpose of the practice simply and effectively. It must also be remembered that children have a short attention span; it is better to demonstrate what you want rather than talking about what you want. Demonstrations rather than words will show a clearer picture to the players and also keep their interest. If you have a practice that is not working, it is far better to stop and revise, or even change it, than to keep on going.

When coaching young players to play soccer, the priority should always be to create a safe learning environment that is not too intense, and one that allows players to develop at their own rate. If young players are allowed to enjoy the game and progress at their own speed, you may just find that they share not only your enthusiasm for the game but your ambitions as well. It has been said that soccer has the greatest range of techniques to be learned of any sport. To encourage mastery of these techniques, the coach and the players must have an enjoyable learning environment and invest not only sufficient time but also patience in the learning process.

We have identified two things that significantly impact a player's performance: coaching and competition. Too much coaching and competition at the wrong time during a player's development could, and often does, lead to failure and disillusionment with the game. This leads some to eventually abandon the game altogether. Our experience and analysis indicate that the most common reasons young players drop out of the sport are an overemphasis on winning, peer pressure, and not enough fun and enjoyment with regards to discovery.

With proper planning, a good soccer coach can make each practice appear new and fresh. This helps build up and recharge the player's interest and enthusiasm for the game. Also, the coach must never lose his or her own enthusiasm, as that enthusiasm will be contagious and will bring out the best in the players.

The duties of a youth coach will vary according to the age of the players under his or her direction. The coach should always set the example for the team by showing and encouraging respect towards opponents and referees. At all times the youth coach should be friendly, fair, punctual, sporting, and enthusiastic about the game. The youngest age-groups should be given only simple, straightforward instructions before or during the game, using language that they can understand. Instruction should also be given clearly at the start of any practice, and feedback given to the players after each session should be constructive rather than overly critical.

As the players' get older, the coach should work on the more complex aspects of the game and extend the players' tactical responsibilities. However, it is essential that the coach retain a balance between striving to improve the knowledge and skills of a group of players while ensuring that they retain their passion and enthusiasm for the game.

For our part, we offer this book and ask that you remember always the need for maximum player-ball contact. Consequently, the practice should always feature the soccer ball—or indeed, soccer balls—prominently. Lastly we remind you, once again, that the most effective practice is one that is well organized, safe, and enjoyable. This ensures that the players learn and remember what has been taught, returning and staying with the sport for many enjoyable years.

Robert "Butch" Lauffer
Alexander "Sandy" Davie

Chapter 1

Basic Principles & Techniques

*H*ere we provide a step-by-step explanation of each skill and technique, including more than one hundred photos, the identification of qualities and methods needed for proper execution, and lists of common faults to watch out for.

The Coach's Reference

The coach will find that the appropriate chapter for the age group—U-8 (under age 8), U-10, U-12, U-15—will serve as the main resource for choosing, planning, and creating practical drills and exercises. Each of these "Drills & Practices" chapters is structured alike with progressive concentration on various techniques and skill developments followed by an emphasis on principles of play and team games.

This first chapter is an encyclopedia of the basic principles, techniques, and skills that will be exercised and called on again and again during practice sessions and games.

Dribbling

Dribbling is the ability of a player to move the ball at a reasonable pace, keeping it close to the feet under pressure from an opponent. Dribbling is one of the most exciting parts of the game of soccer. In a one-on-one or a one-on-two confrontation. A player with good dribbling skills can destroy the best-organized defenses in the world, a superb example of a good dribbler is Brazilian striker Ronaldo. His skill and mastery of the technique mystifies and defies fans and opponents each time he plays. His strength, combined with a sense of touch and close control, an awareness of teammates and opponents, plus speed, and the ability to change direction when running at defenders in the attacking third of the field, make him an outstanding proponent of the skill of dribbling.

Dribbling is a player's way of self-expression during a game. As the game has matured with sophisticated defensive systems of play, we feel that as coaches, we should develop players who have the mentality, technical ability, and bravery to dribble and take on opponents. As coaches we should provide the environment for players to develop this technique so they can learn to handle success and failure. After the player has developed a wide range of feints (deceptions), the coach and player must develop an understanding of when and where to dribble, in what parts of the field, and where to take risks.

Almost all exciting players are good dribblers of the ball, but they run high risks of losing possession. Restrict dribbling in the defending and middle third of the field (1-1) to make space for a pass forward.

The foot surfaces a good dribbler uses are the outside and the inside of the foot (1-2, 1-3). Keep the ball close while scanning the field in between soft touches using the inside and outside parts of each foot just below the midline of the soccer ball.

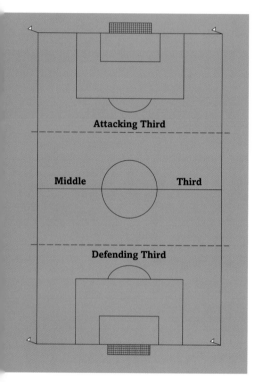

1-1

The Inside of the foot allows the player to push the ball.

The Outside of the foot is used when the player is running at speed.

The Sole of the foot is used to stop the ball or pull it back to change direction.

Dribbling is a means to an end, not an end in itself. The objective is to score, not merely to dribble.

Develop Dribbling in the Attacking Third

Create Pressure Running at opponents.

Penetration Getting behind opponents.

Space for Shooting Deceiving opponents by faking to create space between defending players for a shot.

Qualities of Effective Dribbling

Head up—Awareness Scan the field in between touches. Look at the ball through the bottom half of your eyes. Be aware of teammates and opponents as well as the opening and closing of spaces.

Close Control A player should use either foot to keep the ball within a stride, and be able to change direction quickly without losing the ball to an opponent.

Bent Knees—Balance Keep a low center of gravity; knees must be bent to allow the player to stop, start, accelerate, and change direction.

Change of Direction The player's ability to beat opponents by quick, sharp changes of direction and cutbacks.

Change of Pace The player's ability to use a change of speed to get past opponents.

Feints Use of the body to get the opponent off balance while manipulating the ball with either foot.

Bravery Players must be brave enough to attempt to get past opponents in and around the penalty box, knowing they will probably be kicked or fouled. This mentality will provide great dividends in the form of goals, penalty kicks, and free kicks.

Common Faults

- Head down
- Dribbling with the toe
- Ball too far away
- Attempting to beat the same opponent twice
- Upright stance
- No change of pace or direction
- Running around the ball to turn it

1-3

1-2

Shielding

When shielding the soccer ball, the attacking player should be positioned sideways-on, towards the opponent. The attacker should then form a long barrier by bending the knee and extending the arm closest to the opponent. The other arm should be out for balance, and the ball on the attacker's farthest foot (1-4). Being sideways-on also enables the attacking player to have a bigger field of vision, which will increase the ability to turn.

A common fault is that, when an attacking player attempts to shield the ball flat-on, the player will not be able to make a long barrier. This makes it easier for an opponent to poke the ball away (1-5). This will cut down on the attacker's vision and hinder the ability to turn quickly.

If an opponent challenges from behind, the attacker can then go towards the space that the opponent has left (1-6, 1-7). The attacker can also pivot, change feet, and stay sideways-on to the opponent (1-8, 1-9, 1-10).

1-4

1-5

1-6

1-7

1-9

1-10

1-11

1-12

If an opponent challenges across the face of the attacker, the attacker can pivot and turn away from the opponent (1-11, 1-12), using the inside of the farthest foot to pull the ball from behind and go forward.

Because there are generally more defenders than attackers, it is often necessary that the attackers have the ability to shield the ball well (1-13). This will then create time to allow supporting players to get forward.

Passing

Irrespective of the foot surface being used, the qualities of a good pass are:

Accuracy Playing to feet or in front of a teammate.

Weight Not too hard, not too soft.

Timing Releasing the pass at the appropriate moment.

Disguise Concealing your intention from opponents.

Angle Passing the ball at the correct angle.

1-13

Push Pass

Inside of the Foot

The push pass (kicking the soccer ball with the inside of the foot) is the most accurate method of kicking. It is also the easiest kicking method that a soccer player will learn. The push pass utilizes the largest surface a soccer player has for kicking. The part of the foot used should be from the bottom of the big toe joint area to the bottom half of the arch of the foot. The approach of the player to the ball should be in a straight line (1-14).

1-14

The nonkicking foot should be slightly behind the ball and pointing at the intended target (1-15). The kicking foot should be pointed outward at a right angle with the toe pointing upwards. The foot should be three to five inches off the ground so that the player can strike the ball at the midline or slightly above the midline, enabling the ball to stay on the ground (1-16). Again, the height of the foot will vary depending on the age of the player and the size of the ball used (a 3, 4, or 5). The knee should be bent and the kicking action is from the hip followed by the proper follow-through (1-17).

1-15

1-16

1-17

1-18

The arms are used for balance (1-18). If the player is right-footed, the right arm should be almost straight out from the body. The left arm should be swung out as the kicking leg begins its backswing, and, as it comes forward, the left arm comes back in and across the kicker's chest.

A common fault with very young players is that they will approach the ball from the side and attempt to use the inside of the foot, therefore making it mechanically impossible to pass the ball accurately (1-19).

Another common fault with young players is that when approaching the ball correctly—in a straight line—they may swing their kicking leg across their own body, again making it impossible to kick the ball accurately.

Or they do not open the foot to a right angle and kick the ball on the side; therefore, the ball spins from left to right or right to left, when it should have topspin.

1-19

Swerve Pass

Inside of the Foot

When swerving a pass using the inside of the foot, the approach should be towards the target at an angle not exceeding 45 degrees (1-20).

The nonkicking foot should be approximately 10-12 inches to the side of the ball with the leg slightly bent at the knee. The upper body should be inclined forward slightly, and balance maintained by the arms.

The eyes should be fixed on the ball, off center, where contact is to be made. The backswing of the kicking leg should start simultaneously when taking the final step of the approach (1-21). The leg should be whipped forwards from the hip; on impact, the knee should be slightly bent and the joints held tight (1-22). A low pass or shot will require that contact be made with the ball, off center, through the midline or above.

For a higher trajectory, the upper part of the body leans slightly backwards and the ball should be struck off center and below the midline. The extent of the backwards lean will determine what the player wishes to achieve with the ball.

Following impact, the kicking leg should swing through from the hip (1-23). The backward lean of the upper body should be at its greatest after the follow-through, and straightened as soon as the kicking foot returns to the ground.

1-20

1-21

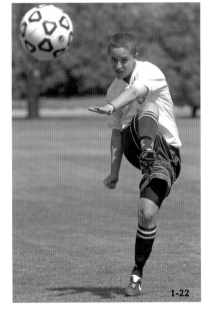

1-22

1-23

Instep Drive (Laces)

The instep drive is the most fluid method of striking a ball. The ball should be struck with the shoelace part of the foot, with the toe pointed down and the ankle locked (1-24). The approach to the ball should be from a slight angle allowing the player a full backswing (1-25). The nonkicking foot should be placed next to the ball and slightly behind it, as well as pointing towards the intended target. The kicking foot knee should be slightly bent during the backswing with the swing motion coming from the hip (1-26). When kicking this way, the player will look up and identify the target, then look down when ready to strike the ball.

After a shot on goal, the player should try to land on the shooting foot; that will allow a full transfer of body weight. The height of the kick will be determined by how far the player moves the body forward over the ball. The knee should be over the ball also. The more forward the body position, the lower the shot will be.

If the player is right-footed, then the right arm should be directly behind the player's body for balance (1-27). The left arm starts out by coming across the chest and proceeds in a counterclockwise motion, ending up behind the body.

1-24

1-25

1-26

1-27

Kicking With the Outside of the Foot

When kicking the ball with the outside of the foot, if approached at an angle, it will go straight; if approached straight on, it will bend or swerve. This method can be used to perform one of three moves:

- Bend the ball into the path of a teammate.
- Bend the ball away from the intended player into space to run onto.
- Bend the ball during a shot on goal.

When the ball is struck with the outside of the foot, the kicking foot should be pointed down and towards the inside of the player with the ankle locked (1-28). The foot should strike the ball off-center, which will make the ball "bend" (1-29).

The knee should be bent, with the kicking action coming from the hip (1-30, 1-31). The follow-through should have the kicking leg come across the player's body (1-32). The nonkicking foot should be 8-10 inches from the ball and slightly behind it.

If the player is kicking with the right foot, then the right arm will stay out to the side of the player for balance. The left arm will start out to the side, and as the player moves forward to kick, the arm will come across the chest.

When shooting on goal, the player should end up on the shooting foot. The transfer of weight onto the front foot will increase the power in the shot. When performing this technique, it is important that the player keep head down and body over the ball.

Common Faults

- Incorrect approach angle
- Nonkicking foot too far away from the ball
- Ankle not locked

1-28

1-29

1-30

1-31

1-32

1-33

Lofted Pass

The lofted pass is a skill used in many aspects of the game of soccer. Goalkeepers use it when taking goal kicks. Defenders use it on occasion when clearing the ball out of a danger area. Attackers are required to use it when crossing the ball into the penalty box, and it is also required when taking corner kicks and free kicks.

The approach to the ball is at an angle so that the player has a full range of motion from the hip (1-33, 1-34). The arm action is the same as for the instep drive. If the kicker is a right-footed player, the right arm should be slightly behind and out to the side of the body for balance (1-35); the left arm starts out coming across the chest and proceeds in a counterclockwise motion, ending up perpendicular with the kicker's body (1-36).

The player's body position should be leaning away and back from the ball, which provides lift. The nonkicking foot should be 8-10 inches to the side and slightly behind the ball.

The toe of the kicking foot should be pointed away from the player, with the ankle locked. The instep of the foot should strike the ball through the bottom half, making it rise. The player should also hit through the middle of the ball to avoid pulling or slicing.

1-34

1-35

1-36

Chipping

When chipping the soccer ball, the approach angle should be straight-on to the ball with the arms out for balance and protection (1-37). The body should be leaning over the ball and the player's head down and locked (1-38). The kicking action should be a sharp, descending jab from the knee with very little or no follow-through (1-39). The point of contact should be the top of the toe area of the kicking foot, striking completely below the ball. This kicking action will provide a sharp vertical trajectory over a short distance.

This particular type of skill can be used to get over and/or behind opponents when other passing alternatives are not available.

Common Faults

- Head raised too early
- Failure to get under the ball
- Kicking the ground
- Toe punting
- Using the whole leg
- A long follow-through

Full Volleys

A full volley is a kicking method where the player kicks the ball before it touches the ground. This technique can be performed in one of two ways: either by approaching down the line of flight of the ball or across the line of flight of the ball.

Striking at the Goal—Inside of the Foot Volley

The approach should be down the line of flight of the ball. The nonkicking foot should be pointing towards the intended target. The knee of the nonkicking leg should be slightly flexed to give balance and stability (1-40). The kicking action starts with the lifting and opening up of the kicking leg from the hip. The knee should be locked, with the final kicking action coming from the knee down, where the lower leg is stiff. The contact foot should be at a right angle with the ankle locked (1-41). The foot strikes the ball at the midline or slightly above to keep it low. The follow-through should be short and towards the target.

The body should be upright and slightly leaning back. Arms should be extended out and almost shoulder high for balance, composure, and protection. The head should be steady and the eyes fixed firmly on the ball.

1-40

1-41

Attacking—Instep Volley (Laces)

The approach should be down the line of flight of the ball. The nonkicking foot should be pointing towards the intended target. The knee of the nonkicking leg should be slightly flexed for balance and stability. The kicking action starts with the raising of the knee of the kicking foot (1-42). The final kicking action should occur from the knee down, with the lower leg stiff. The toes of the contact foot should be pointing towards the ground with the ankle locked and the knee over the top of the ball (1-43).

The laces of the shoe should make contact with the center of the ball at the midline or slightly above to keep the ball low. The body should be upright and leaning slightly forward. Arms should be out and almost shoulder high; the head should be steady and the eyes firmly fixed on the ball.

Common Faults

- Head up
- Failure to get knee over the ball
- Leaning back
- Kicking the ball off center
- Failure to land on the shooting foot
- Failure to keep the toe pointing down

1-42

1-43

1-44

Attacking—Outside of the Foot Volley

The approach should be down the line of flight of the ball. The nonkicking foot should be pointing towards the intended target (1-44). The knee of the nonkicking leg should be slightly flexed to give balance and stability (1-45). The kicking action starts with the raising of the knee from the hip of the kicking foot (1-46). The knee should be brought across the thigh of the nonkicking leg, and the toe of the kicking foot should be pointed down and inward towards the kicker. Contact should be made from the area of the small toe to midway down the outside of the foot.

The attacker, depending on the power needed, may land on the kicking foot. The body should be upright with the left arm starting outward from the body and coming across the chest. The right arm should be out, hanging down for balance (1-47). The ball should be struck through left of center at the midline; if left-footed, the opposite will apply. Striking the ball off center will make it swerve.

Defending—Full Volley

When players use the technique of a full volley for defending purposes, there are a few points to consider.

1-45

1-46

1-47

1-48

Defending—Inside of the Foot Volley

When defending, the technique of the inside of the foot volley has similarities to that of the attacking volley in that the approach should still be down the line of flight of the ball. The kicking action should be the same, the main differences being that when the foot strikes the ball, it should be underneath the midline (1-49), with the player leaning well back to give it height (1-50).

Defending—Instep Volley

The two major differences of the instep volley when defending are:

- The knee should not be over the ball (1-51).
- The foot should make contact below the ball (1-52).
- A combination of these two principles as well as the player leaning back will ensure that the ball goes either high or far (1-53).

1-49

1-50

1-51

1-52

1-53

Common Faults

- The nonkicking foot not pointing at goal
- Player taking eyes off the ball
- Leaning back
- Striking underneath the ball
- Ankle not locked

Attacking–Inside of the Foot Volley–Across the Line

When shooting on goal with the inside of the foot, the player's nonkicking foot must be pointing towards the target, not past it.

The initial foot position will allow the player to open up and face the ball down its line of flight. This body position will allow the correct kicking technique. The movement starts with the knee being raised until the inside of the foot becomes level with the middle of the ball (1-54).

The kicking action is initiated from the hip, as the whole leg is brought across the player's body and the flight of the ball (1-55). The lower leg should be stiff, ankle locked, and toe pointed upward. The arms are up and out for balance, head steady and eyes looking at the ball.

With young players, have them concentrate on preparing to receive the ball early, and then watch it hit and leave their foot.

1-54

1-55

Attacking–Instep Volley–Across the Line

Goals scored from full volleys attacking across the line of flight of the ball can be both exciting and spectacular. However, some attempts to do so can, and do, go astray. The preparation of the player before contact is made with the ball is one of the most important parts of performing this technique.

The player's back should be turned virtually towards the goal that is being attacked, as the player plants and pivots on the foot nearest to the goal, pointing it towards the target (1-56). The leading shoulder should drop down to allow the kicking leg to swing smoothly, enabling the player to strike over and through the ball, keeping the shot low and on target (1-57). The player's ankle must be locked and the toe pointed away from the player (1-58).

It is essential that the player's head be steady, keeping the eyes on the ball until contact is made. The player should follow through and land on the shooting foot.

1-58

1-56

1-57

Common Faults

- Planting the nonkicking foot in front of or past the ball
- Taking eyes off the ball
- Leaning back
- Striking underneath the ball
- Striking the ball straight-on and not sideways-on to the target

- Head up
- Underestimating the flight of the ball
- Ankle not locked
- Failure to lean back
- Striking too far over the ball

Defending–Inside of the Foot & Instep Volleys–Across the Line

When defending, the inside volley (1-59) and the instep volley (1-60) have similarities to that of the attacking techniques. The two major differences are:

- Leaning well back
- Striking underneath the ball

    Adopting both these principles will ensure height and distance.

1-59

1-60

Attacking—Half Volley

When does a half volley occur? It occurs when a player's reflexes are not quick enough to permit a strike on the ball before it hits the ground.

The main differences between the half volley and the full volley are that in the half volley the kicking foot strikes the ball as it contacts the ground. The half volley has a much lower and faster trajectory than the full volley, therefore, having the advantage of reaching the target faster.

Half-volley shooting chances occur from bouncing or dropping balls, lofted forward passes, corners, free kicks, and rebounds from the goal area (1-61). In most cases the attacking player will come in and meet the ball down its line of flight (1-62). The player should make contact with the laces of the shoe slightly above the midline of the ball with the ankle locked and the toe pointing down (1-63). The knee should be bent and over the ball with the body leaning forward; this will keep the shot low. The head is steady, eyes on the ball; arms are down and slightly bent for balance and protection; the follow-through is a short punch-like action. The nonkicking foot should be alongside the ball and pointing towards the target; if it is behind the ball, the shot will go high.

1-61

1-62

1-63

Control Surfaces

The most common parts of the body used to control the ball are:

- Inside of the foot
- Outside of the foot
- Instep
- Sole of the foot
- Thigh
- Lower abdomen—when the ball bounces
- Chest
- Head

Control becomes a skill when the player selects the correct controlling surface at the right tactical time.

Ground & Aerial Control

The definition of control in soccer is "a player's ability to gain possession of a moving ball so that it can be shielded, dribbled, passed or shot." The player should identify the flight path, keep eyes on the ball, select and move the controlling surface into its line of flight as early as possible, then relax and withdraw that surface on contact to produce a "cushion effect."

In today's game there is very rarely time to bring the ball to a complete standstill; therefore, the ball should be taken into stride without stopping. The receiving player's concentration should be divided between the ball and the opposition; when controlling the ball, the player's first touch is vitally important (1-64). Many times the first touch (or lack of first touch) may cause the player to:

- Lose possession of the ball.
- Miss scoring opportunities.
- Risk injury in attempting to regain possession.

Principles of Control

1. Identify the flight path.
2. Eyes on the ball.
3. Select the controlling surface of the body as early as possible and move it into the line of flight of the ball.
4. Relax the controlling surface on contact, or even withdraw it slightly.
5. Control the ball for shielding, dribbling, passing, or shooting.
6. Observe teammates, opponents, and the target area.

When controlling a dropping ball it is important that the player gets underneath it, and does not allow it to bounce, as this will allow more time and space to make the best tactical decision or correct any error. Young players can be guilty of allowing the ball one bounce before attempting to control it. It is true that it is easier to control the ball following the first bounce. However, this will give an opponent time to close down space, pressure the controlling player, and possibly dispossess the player of the ball if the surface is uneven and the ball bounces towards the opponent.

NOTE: When the basic principles of control are understood by young players, a progression towards moving situations in practice should be implemented to simulate game conditions.

Ground Control—Inside of the Foot

The inside of the foot is the surface most used to control a ball rolling along the ground.

At times a player will have to move forwards, backwards, or sideways to receive the ball. When a player receives a ball, it has to be controlled cleanly; this allows the player to shield, dribble, pass, or shoot.

With eyes fixed firmly on the ball, the nonkicking leg bent, and the arms out for balance, the player should relax and withdraw the inside of the controlling foot slightly to take the pace off the ball as it is received (1-64). Often, holding the joints too tightly can cause the ball to rebound away from the player. The toe should be raised and the ankle locked, with the controlling foot at a right angle. The leg should be turned outwards from the hip and the knee bent.

It is important to remember that the controlling foot should be raised so that it meets the ball at its midline or slightly above. This will keep the ball on the ground. If the controlling foot is not raised, the ball will pop up in the air off the player's foot, making it harder to control; a good defender will use that "air time" to his or her advantage and curtail the attacker's options (1-65).

1-64

1-65

Ground Control—Outside of the Foot

When controlling the ball with the outside of the foot, the player's nonkicking leg should be slightly bent at the knee, with the upper body leaning back (1-66). The arms should be down and away for balance and the eyes fixed firmly on the ball. The controlling leg should be bent as it moves to gather the ball, with the controlling foot raised and pointing inwards. If the ball is played too far away from the player's line of approach, it may be necessary to have the controlling leg come all the way across the nonkicking leg.

Controlling with the outside of the foot can be used to a player's advantage to gain time by playing the ball away from an opponent (1-67). This can create time and space in which to shoot, pass, or dribble (1-68).

Ground Control & Turning—Inside of the Foot

When controlling and turning with the inside of the foot, the player should move towards the ball and position the nonkicking foot alongside it (1-69).

When the controlling foot meets the ball, the player should pivot to the inside on the nonkicking foot (1-70). At the same time, the controlling foot should be withdrawn, allowing the ball to roll through as the player performs a 180-degree turn (1-71).

1-66

1-67

1-68

1-69

1-70

1-71

Another method is with the player approaching the ball sideways-on. This increases vision when checking away from an opponent. This type of control and turn is executed mainly by forwards attempting to create space for scoring opportunities against tight-marking defenders (1-72).

The player should approach the ball and plant the nonkicking foot alongside it. The ball should roll and meet the controlling surface underneath the player (1-73, 1-74). Using the inside of the foot, the ball is guided behind the nonkicking leg while the player pivots on the nonkicking foot to continue the movement (1-75).

Ground Control & Turning—Outside of the Foot

To control with the outside of the foot, the player must first calculate the pace of the ball. This will determine whether to go meet it. If the player judges to stay, because the ball has been played firmly, then the receiving player will only have to redirect it by using the outside of the foot while turning (1-76). If the player goes forward to meet the ball, the nonkicking foot should be planted alongside it as the turning foot is extended forward to make contact. This foot should be raised and pointed inward so that it redirects the path of the ball with the outside of the foot (1-77), enabling the player to control and turn in one movement (1-78, 1-79).

1-75

1-72 · 1-73 · 1-74 · 1-76 · 1-77 · 1-78 · 1-79

Ground Control—Sole of the Foot

When controlling the ball using the sole of the foot, the player should move forward to trap it with the ball of the foot (1-80). The controlling leg should be bent and the foot held at a 45-degree angle to the ground. After contact, the player must keep the weight on the noncontrolling leg to maintain balance.

Aerial Control—Inside of the Foot

One method of controlling a ball of medium height and flight path is to use the inside of the foot. With eyes on the ball, the player should move the controlling surface into its line of flight (1-81). Keeping the body in an upright position and the arms out for balance, the nonkicking foot should be pointing towards the direction of the ball. The controlling leg should be lifted and turned out from the hip, forward of the player, so that when contact is made it can be withdrawn (1-82). The ankle joint should be locked to take the pace off the ball and ensure that it drops down. The inside of the foot should make contact through the midline of the ball.

1-80

1-81

1-82

Aerial Control—Instep

With the head steady and eyes fixed firmly on the ball, the player should move into and underneath the line of flight of the ball. The controlling leg should be raised from the hip with the toe pointing away, ankle relaxed, and the knee bent (1-83).

Contact between the ball and instep should be made at about knee height. The noncontrolling leg should be bent slightly at the knee, and the arms held out for balance (1-84). The controlling leg should descend rapidly, moving downwards in the beginning almost at the same pace as the ball. As it gets nearer to the ground, the speed of descent should be slower.

This will allow the longest possible contact with the instep, and ensure that the pace will be taken off the ball.

1-83

Aerial Control—Thigh

The player must get underneath and in line with the ball, raise the controlling leg from the hip, and bend the knee. If the flight path of the ball is relatively low, the thigh should point obliquely to the ground. If the ball is falling from a higher trajectory, then the thigh should be moved into a horizontal position (1-85). The soft or upper part of the thigh should make contact with the ball before being withdrawn (1-86). Because of the density of the upper thigh, this contact will take the pace off the ball. The noncontrolling leg should be slightly bent and the player's eyes fixed firmly on the ball, with the arms out for balance.

1-84

1-85

1-86

1-87

Aerial Control—Lower Abdomen

Once in line with the flight of the ball, the player can use the stomach or abdomen to control the ball following an awkward bounce from the ground (1-87).

In most cases, a player can apply this technique when reflexes or reactions were too slow prior to the bounce.

At the moment of contact, the stomach should be firm with the legs straight, while at the same time the upper part of the body leans forward from the hips and over the ball. The arms should be held down and away from the body.

Aerial Control—Chest

When controlling the ball with the chest, the plane of the chest is dependent on the arc of the ball. If the ball is driven hard and straight, the player should move into the line of the flight (1-88), pulling the chest away at the moment of contact to cushion the impact (1-89).

If the ball is dropping from a high arc, a wide stance should be taken, allowing the player's chest to get into a horizontal position. Keeping the eyes on the ball, the player should move the controlling surface underneath and into its line of flight (1-90). A wide stance will allow the player to bend the knees, push forward with the hips, and lean back, positioning the chest to receive the ball (1-91). The arms should be out for balance.

1-88

1-89

1-90

1-91

As a guide, the player can use the chin to line up the ball and chest correctly (1-92). As the ball drops, have the chin aiming at it, then at the last moment pull the head back (1-93). The ball should land correctly on the chest. Once contact has been made, the ball should be brought to the ground as quickly as possible (1-94, 1-95, 1-96). The angle of impact and rebound are identical when performing this technique.

1-94

1-92

1-93

1-95

1-96

Tackling

Tackling is a technical and tactical tool in the game of soccer. The technique of tackling is taking the ball directly away from an opponent. The tactical element is the continual consideration of when to tackle and how to tackle. Opportunities to tackle are:

① When the ball is in between the feet of the attacker.

② When the ball is too far away from the attacker.

③ When the attacker has made a bad first touch.

④ In some cases, the defender may have to delay the opponent and wait for a chance to win the ball.

When tackling, the defender should be positioned about a yard from the attacker, using a staggered stance. The foot should be swung backwards, as when kicking with the inside of the foot, except that the backswing is shorter (1-97). As the foot comes forward, the muscles and joints should be tightened and the foot placed in front of the ball to act as an obstacle.

When the foot makes contact with the ball, the trunk should be inclined slightly forward and balance maintained by the arms. In order to tackle more powerfully, the tackling foot should be pushed forward on contact.

1-97

Heading

Heading is an important technique every outfield player should master. When heading, the player should use the forehead, and nod firmly through the ball in the direction of the target. Do not just allow the ball to hit the head.

Heading-Feet on the Ground

When heading from the ground, the player should arch the body and tighten the neck (1-98). The feet should be spaced apart, forming a good base, with the eyes fixed on the ball until impact. The mouth should be closed, and the arms out for balance and protection. The trunk should move forward to give strength to the heading action and the forehead should meet the ball hard, putting power into the header (1-99).

Point of contact between the head and the ball can vary depending on whether the player is in an attacking or defending situation. If heading to score—attacking—the point of contact between the forehead and the ball should be above and through the midline, to keep the ball down (1-100).

If heading to clear—defending—the point of contact should be below the midline allowing the player height, distance, and time (1-101).

If the player intends to head the ball sideways, the trunk should be rotated in the required direction so that the surface of the forehead and the trunk are at a right angle, towards the direction the player wishes the ball to go.

Heading-Feet off the Ground

When the ball has to be headed with the feet off the ground, the player can use either of the following methods:

- Running one-footed takeoff
- Standing two-footed takeoff

If the player is going to use these, the considerations are:

- Timing of the jump
- Heading the ball at the highest point in the jump

1-98

1-99

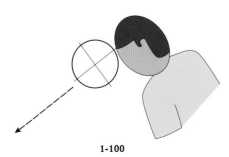

1-100

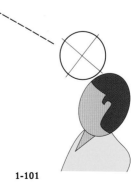

1-101

1-102

1-103

1-104

Heading—One-Footed Takeoff

When using a running one-footed takeoff, the player should use an approach run of five to eight yards. During the run-up, it is important that the player does not change pace, as this will cause loss of both speed in the approach and height in the jump.

On takeoff, the knee and ankle of the takeoff leg should push upwards and straighten out. The arms should come through and up with the non-takeoff leg bent at the knee and driving upwards.

The action of the arms and non-takeoff leg will help the player to achieve maximum height. At the point of takeoff, the upper body should be leaning forward.

When the player reaches maximum height, the body should lean backwards, then move forwards. With the eyes focused on the ball and the neck firm, the forehead should meet the ball with a thrusting action; this will provide the follow-through. The player should land on both feet.

If the player is heading in an attacking situation, the ball should be struck above the midline, enabling it to be played downwards. For defending purposes, the ball must be headed below the midline to achieve distance, height, and time.

Heading—Two-Footed Takeoff

The player should start the jumping action by planting the feet, either staggered or parallel, 8-10 inches apart. The arms should be swung backwards and the knees slightly bent, with the upper body leaning forward.

The arms should then be swung forwards and upwards with the legs straightening out and the feet pushing off the ground (1-102). The upper body should move backwards and then thrust forwards to allow the forehead to meet the ball (1-103). The player should end up landing on both feet.

If the player intends to change the direction of the ball, the trunk should be rotated towards the intended direction of play immediately after takeoff (1-104).

Goalkeeping

The dictionary defines the word "goalkeeper" in soccer as a player who protects the goal. Certainly, keeping the ball out of the net is the primary objective, but there is more to goalkeeping than just stopping shots.

Communication with and organization of the players on the team are two of the hidden strengths that a goalkeeper can use to help prevent dangerous situations from developing. The goalkeeper's ability to read these situations is not always appreciated, as all that people see are the shots that are saved—and not saved.

The goalkeeper is the only team member who is allowed to use hands as well as feet; therefore, they must possess the athleticism of a gymnast (1-105), be the last line of defense, and be the instigator of attacks. It is therefore surprising that despite their importance, goalkeepers are often neglected during coaching sessions.

Here we illustrate that there is no mystery to goalkeeping; efficiency is based on correct decision-making and technique.

Starting Position

The goalkeeper's feet should be shoulder width apart, the knees slightly bent to bring the body weight forward onto the front part of the feet (1-106). The arms should be to the side of the body with the hands waist high. The head should be steady and tilted slightly forward with the eyes fixed firmly on the ball.

1-106

1-105

1-107

Basic Handling—Ground Shots

When the goalkeeper has time to get the whole body behind the ball there are two basic techniques for stopping ground shots:

Stoop Technique The feet should be directly behind the ball, close enough together not to allow the ball to go through the legs (1-107). The arms should be down with the hands behind the ball and the palms facing outwards, to enable the ball to be scooped upwards and into the chest (1-108). The head should be steady with the eyes on the ball.

Kneeling Technique The feet and lower body should be sideways-on to the ball, with the knee of the kneeling leg alongside the heel of the other leg. The trunk should be turned so that the shoulders are facing square-on towards the ball (1-109). The arms should be down with the hands behind the ball and the palms facing outwards. The head should be steady with the eyes on the ball (1-110). With this technique, the goalkeeper should be able to scoop the ball in toward the chest and stand up (1-111, 1-112).

However, if balance is lost, the goalkeeper should drop forward, pinning the ball to the ground between the arms and the chest (1-113).

1-108

1-109

1-110

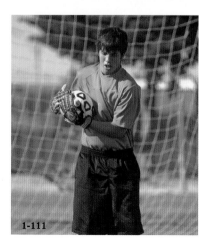
1-111

1-112

1-113

Handling—Waist-High Shots

The starting position is as described above with the head steady and the eyes on the ball. The palms of the hands should be facing outwards to cup the ball into the waist (1-114), while the upper body folds over to secure it (1-115).

Handling—Chest Shots

The starting position is as described above with the head steady and the eyes on the ball. The palms of the hands should be facing outwards to cup the ball into the chest. On impact, the chest should be relaxed so that the ball can be trapped firmly between the hands and chest (1-116).

Handling—Head-High & Above Shots

The staring position is as described above with the head steady and the eyes fixed firmly on the ball. The hands should be behind and to the side of the ball. The fingers should be spread and relaxed, forming a "W" (1-117).

Once the ball has been caught, it should be brought quickly down into the body to protect it from opponents. When handling shots above the head, the goalkeeper should push upwards off one leg to gain maximum height in the jump and give protection against a challenge from opponents (1-118).

1-114

1-115

1-116

1-117

1-118

Diving—Shots Near the Body

These are difficult to save, especially if they are on the ground. The leg closest to the ball should collapse quickly (1-119), enabling the lower body to get out of the way so that the upper body and hands can stop the ball (1-120).

Diving—Shots Away From the Body

The correct technique is to move the body weight onto the leg nearest the ball and thrust off that leg when making the save (1-121).

Diving—Vision

To avoid obstruction of vision, the goalkeeper should dive sideways-on with the arms positioned so that they are outside the line of vision (1-122). Do not allow the goalkeeper to dive facedown, as this will impair vision.

1-119

1-120

1-121

1-122

Chapter 2

Injury Management

A collision in the sport of soccer can sometimes result in injury. There are other dangers, too. Our intent with this chapter is to help lessen the chance of injuries to players, as well as provide basic first-aid procedures. Preventative measures are a major part of any sport, and should be incorporated into your program. Maintaining fluids, guarding against and recognizing heat illnesses, and providing adequate warm-up through stretching are important methods of preventing problems that could become acute.

2-1 Hamstrings

2-2 Quadriceps

2-3 Groins

Stretching

Stretching is important prior to strenuous activity, and is essential to prevent injury. Stretching after practice or competition is just as important since it helps reduce soreness and encourages good muscle recovery. **Players Should Warm Up** to maximize practice time by engaging in light exercise with the ball. This will increase the blood flow to the muscles, as well as warm them and prepare them for stretching. Never stretch a cold muscle. Once the body is sweating freely, all major muscle groups should be stretched:

- Quadriceps (2-1)
- Hamstrings (2-2)
- Groins (2-3)
- Calves (2-4)
- Lower back (2-5, 2-6)

Cold sprays, cooling gels, and anti-inflammatory preparations can be used on injured muscles. They can decrease pain and aid in an increased range of motion.

Before practice or a game, a light stretching regimen should be followed once the body is sweating freely, and also afterwards to cool the body down. This will help increase flexibility and decrease muscle soreness and tightness.

Fluids

Before training or a game, the body should be prehydrated by drinking eight to ten cups of water. This will saturate the body tissues and give the body a reserve to draw from as it perspires. Remember that when the body sweats, it loses more than just water—it loses iron, trace minerals, and calcium. These are important to the muscles to keep them functioning normally.

During the match or practice, water should be supplied every 15 to 20 minutes to avoid dehydration. Cold water is preferred to quench thirst. When it is very humid outside, water must be replaced even more frequently.

Electrolyte drinks will also replace these essential elements. If a person wants to ingest them while playing, it is recommended that the drinks be diluted with water as they have a tendency to upset the stomach when consumed during intense exercise.

Heat Illnesses

Heat Cramps are the first sign of dehydration. Any player who suffers cramps should be removed from the field immediately and encouraged to drink cold fluids. Lightly stretching and massaging the muscles involved will help to alleviate the problem more quickly.

Heat Exhaustion is a serious condition caused by the loss of body fluids. The person may seem disoriented and will sweat profusely and the skin will become flushed. Lay the casualty down in a cool place. Apply iced towels if available. If the player is conscious, give sips of cold water to drink and seek medical aid.

Heat Stroke is a medical emergency. Initial signs and symptoms are that the skin will be dry and clammy. At this stage, the player loses the ability to sweat and the kidneys can shut down. The player will be disoriented or possibly unconscious. Someone should call 911 or the local emergency number immediately.

For All Heat Illnesses remove the person from the elements to an area of shade. The person should be given cold water unless unconscious. Ice bags or cold towels should be put behind the neck, under armpits, on elbows, and behind the knees.

Restrictive clothing should be loosened or removed to allow air to get to the skin. A cool, damp cloth should be rubbed over the skin to promote evaporation.

2-4   Calves

2-5/2-6   Lower Back

Nosebleeds

Besides resulting from impacts, nosebleeds can also be caused by a combination of overheating and dehydration. The person should be placed in a shaded or air-conditioned area. Blood flow can be restricted by pinching the bridge of the nose (2-7). Place a pad under the nose to catch the blood. Do not tilt the head back; this causes the blood to drain into the stomach, causing nausea. Instead, lean them forward while placing an ice pack over the nose to quicken blood-clotting.

2-7

Shin Splints

Shin splints are characterized by very sharp, shooting pains down the shins. This condition has a slow onset, but it soon becomes debilitating. Rest and ice are the most important aids in overcoming this injury.

Help Prevent Shin Splints by supporting the arches of the feet and stretching the calves. If the condition persists, consult a physician. Chronic shin splints can result in stress fractures.

Flesh Wounds

With all flesh wounds, monitor them for signs of infection. Redness, warmth, and a pus-like discharge are signs that require additional medical attention.

Simple Abrasion is best treated by washing the area with soap and water, and leaving it open. Application of a triple antibiotic ointment and covering the wound is recommended during competition.

Laceration is treated by placing a sterile gauze pad or clean cloth over the wound and applying direct pressure to slow the bleeding. Ice will also help the blood to clot. For deep cuts to the skin, stitches may be required. Seek medical attention if warranted.

Do Not Use a Tourniquet as this will cut off the blood supply and could cause tissue to die.

Suspect the Worst

The most important concept is, always suspect the worst in the event of an injury.

Protect the player by removing the person from the field. If an injury requires a splint, use anything, from two boards to a couple of rolled-up newspapers. Splint the injured part to immobilize the area and protect it from additional incidental injury. If using tape or cloth straps, secure them, but not so tightly as to restrict blood flow. Just tighten enough to keep the injured area immobile until the person is able to seek further medical attention. Commercial splints are preferable if available.

Rest, keeping the weight off the injured area to prevent complicating the injury.

Ice the area by applying an ice pack. Remember, ice packs should never be applied directly to the skin. A damp cloth should cover the area to prevent a skin reaction to the ice.

Ice should always be used on a new injury, as it will slow down the swelling by reducing the blood flow to the area. Ice should not be used on an old injury before activity.

Ice should be applied for a minimum of 15 to 20 minutes. Before reapplying the ice, allow 20 to 30 minutes for the area to warm up again. Ice treatment should continue for up to 72 hours after the injury. All swelling should be over by this time.

Compress as needed to reduce swelling.

Elevate the limb or body as needed to control the blood flow.

The P.R.I.C.E. Principle is an easy acronym to remember:

Protect to prevent against further injury.

Rest to avoid further complications.

Ice to control pain and swelling.

Compress to reduce swelling.

Elevate to control the blood flow.

Chapter 3

U-8 Drills & Practices

(under age 8)

A t this age level, focus team play on small-sided games; one-on-one through three-on-three. Place the emphasis on active, fun soccer, allowing many touches on the ball while introducing and developing basic techniques—dribbling, kicking, control, and heading.

Once every four weeks, expose each of the players to the goalkeeping position. This will help each player develop an overall, well-balanced perspective of the goalkeeper's role.

Warm-up 10 minutes
Technique Introduction
10 minutes
Skill Development
10 minutes
Team Game 10-15 minutes
Free Play 10-20 minutes

Practices

WARM-UP

FIELD SIZE 15-yd x 15-yd grid.

ORGANIZATION 10 players, each with a soccer ball; four cones. All the players are dribbling their ball inside the grid (3-1). The coach shouts out a part of the body that each player has to use to stop the ball, e.g., the sole of the right foot, the left knee, etc.

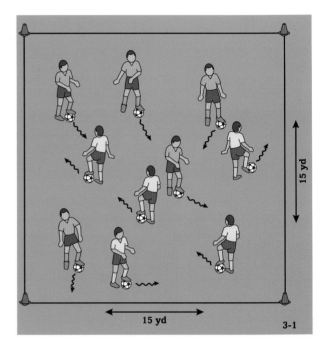

15 yd

15 yd

3-1

Coaching Points

- Do not allow players to run in straight lines or circles.
- Encourage players to zigzag.
- Keep the players moving.
- Have players keep the head up.
- Emphasize close control.
- Don't allow toe-kicking.

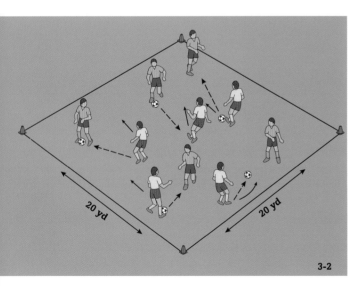

20 yd

20 yd

3-2

WARM-UP

FIELD SIZE 20-yd x 20-yd grid.

ORGANIZATION 10 players, groups of two, with one soccer ball per group. Have each group pass and receive with the inside of the foot (3-2).

PROGRESSION Restrict players to two touches.

Coaching Points

- Use the correct kicking surface.
- Get in line to receive the ball.
- Move after the pass.
- Accuracy—weight and timing of the pass.

DRIBBLING

FIELD SIZE 20-yd x 20-yd grid.

ORGANIZATION 10 players, each with a soccer ball; four cones. Everyone dribbles around the grid (3-3). The objective: the players try to kick everyone else's soccer ball out of the grid, while keeping their own ball protected.

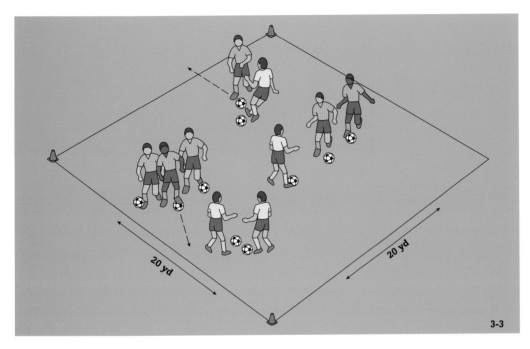

20 yd

20 yd

3-3

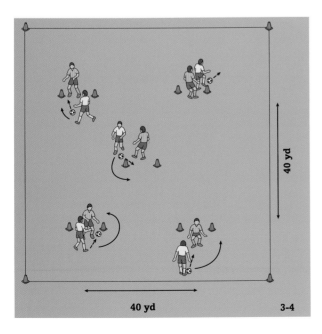

40 yd

40 yd

3-4

DRIBBLING

FIELD SIZE 40-yd x 40-yd grid.

ORGANIZATION 10 players, groups of two, one soccer ball per group, 14 cones. Use 10 cones to make five small goals, 1½ yards wide (3-4). Put a group at each goal and have them play one-on-one, dribbling towards their group's own goal. Each player can score only through their side of their own goal.

DRIBBLING

FIELD SIZE 20-yd x 20-yd grid.

ORGANIZATION 10 players, each with a soccer ball; four cones. Each player dribbles a ball around inside the grid. On the coach's command, the player has to stop the ball by placing a foot on top of it. As soon as the ball is stationary, the player moves off to collect a teammate's ball and continues dribbling around the area until the next command to change (3-5).

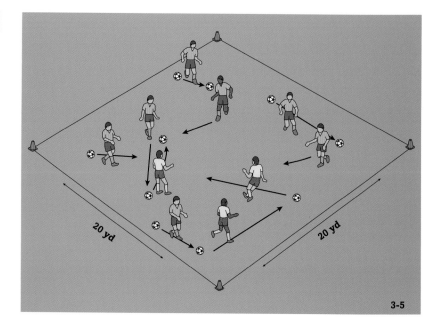

3-5

DRIBBLING

FIELD SIZE 20-yd x 20-yd grid.

TIME One to two minutes, then change.

ORGANIZATION 10 players, two teams of five, five soccer balls, five bibs. One team, without soccer balls, stands anywhere inside the grid, with legs apart. The other team's players each have a soccer ball. On the coach's command, each player with a soccer ball is to dribble and play the ball through the legs of the other team's player (3-6). Each time a player does this, a point is awarded. The object is to see how many points each team can accumulate during the allotted time. The only restriction is that the dribbling player cannot go back through the same set of legs without going through another set first.

3-6

ONE-ON-ONE

FIELD SIZE 30-yd x 20-yd grid.

ORGANIZATION 10 players, two teams of five—four outfield players and one goalkeeper—six cones, five bibs. Keepers should be rotated every 10 shots. Each outfield player should be numbered one to four. The coach plays the ball between the two teams and shouts a number, the designated player on each team runs out and battles to win the ball, with the winner attempting to dribble and score (3-7).

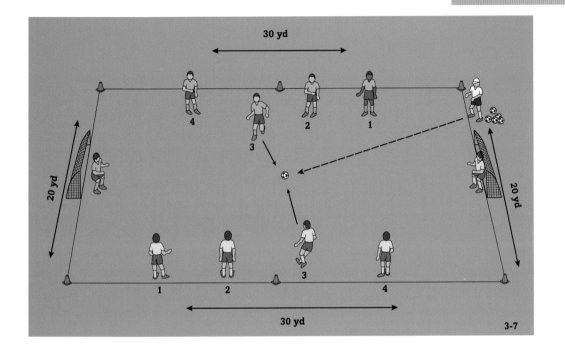

3-7

PASSING—INSIDE OF THE FOOT *(Individual)*

ORGANIZATION One player, one soccer ball. From a distance of five to ten yards, kick or pass the ball against a wall using the inside of the foot. Attempt to keep the ball below an imaginary line with consecutive passes (3-8). Variations on this theme can be achieved by using the instep or outside of the foot.

3-8

ORGANIZATION 10 players in groups of two, one soccer ball per group, 10 cones. The practice is set up where two cones are placed two yards apart, with each player five yards from the cones. Both players must pass the ball back and forth through the cones using two touches (3-9). After achieving some proficiency, turn the practice into a game where each group of two plays against all the other groups, e.g., see how many successful passes can be made in one minute. All passes must go through the cones cleanly.

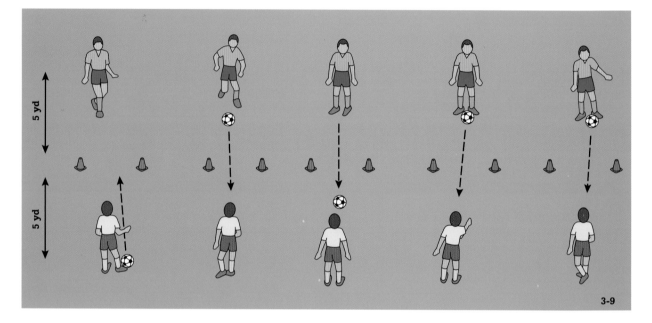

3-9

PASSING—INSIDE OF THE FOOT

ORGANIZATION 10 players, two groups of five, one soccer ball, two cones. Place the cones two yards apart in the middle, and the two groups of five on each side of the cones; play the ball through the cones using two touches. The player follows the pass to the other line (3-10). To make this into a competitive game, have the teams complete a number of successful passes against the clock, e.g., 20 passes in three minutes.

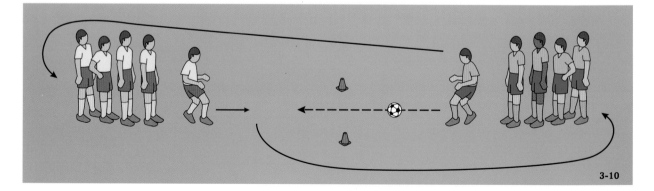

3-10

PASSING—INSIDE OF THE FOOT

ORGANIZATION 10 players, five groups of two, one soccer ball per group, 11 cones. Set up five grids, 10 yds × 10 yds each. Have a group in each grid, passing and moving; they are to keep the ball inside the grid, using the inside of the foot (3-11).

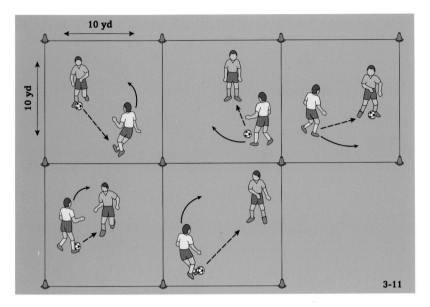

10 yd

10 yd

3-11

PASSING—OUTSIDE OF THE FOOT

FIELD SIZE 50 yds × 20 yds.

ORGANIZATION 10 players, five soccer balls, 22 cones. Each player has a partner, with one ball between the two of them. Pass the ball through the cones set out two yards apart, using the outside of the foot. Start the practice with the players five to six yards away from the cones, and increase the distance as the players become more successful (3-12).

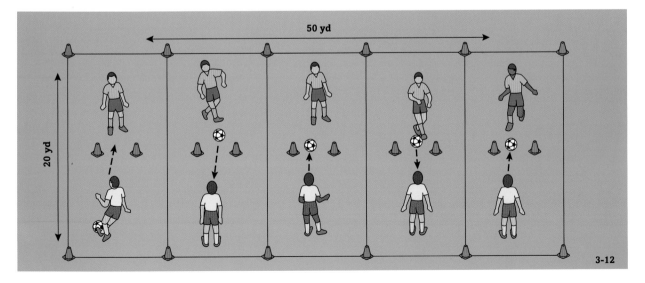

50 yd

20 yd

3-12

PASSING—OUTSIDE OF THE FOOT

FIELD SIZE 20-yd x 20-yd grid.

ORGANIZATION 10 players, five soccer balls, four cones. In twos, each pair moves around inside the grid, passing the ball back and forth to each other using the outside of the foot (3-13).

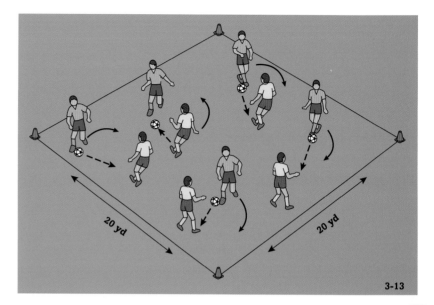

3-13

PASSING—OUTSIDE OF THE FOOT

ORGANIZATION 10 players plus a goalkeeper, five soccer balls, four cones. Five players on the goal line, the others along the edge of the penalty area. Goalkeeper in goal. Work in pairs: the player on the goal line plays a ball diagonally across the penalty area to a partner who strikes the ball using the outside of the foot in an attempt to score. After the shot, the player retrieves the ball while the passer advances to the edge of the penalty area (3-14).

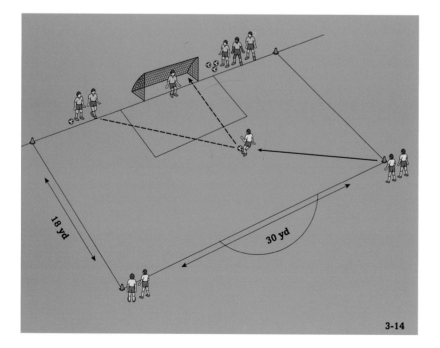

3-14

Coaching Points

- Nonkicking foot 8-10 inches from the ball, and slightly behind it.
- Kicking foot pointed down and inwards.
- Kicking-foot knee bent, and kicking action from the hip.
- Strike ball off center.
- Head down, body over the ball to keep the ball low.
- Instep drive

INSTEP DRIVE

FIELD SIZE 50 yds x 20 yds.

ORGANIZATION 10 players, 22 cones, five soccer balls, one ball shared between two players. Each player attempts to play the ball through two cones spaced two yards apart, using the instep drive. Starting distance from the cones should be approximately five to six yards, increasing to 10 yards as progress is made (3-15).

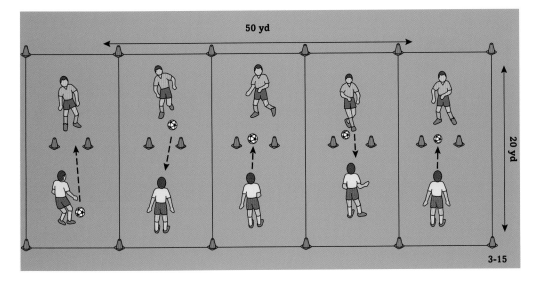

INSTEP DRIVE

ORGANIZATION 10 players plus a goalkeeper, five soccer balls, seven cones. Place the cones in an arc approximately 10 yards from goal. Five teams of two are selected. One player from each pair should be situated at the goalpost with the ball, the other behind the first set of cones in the arc. Using the inside of the foot, the player on the post passes the ball between each set of cones in turn; the other partner attempts to score with an instep drive (3-16). Each time a score is made, the scorer retrieves the ball while his or her partner proceeds to the next set of cones.

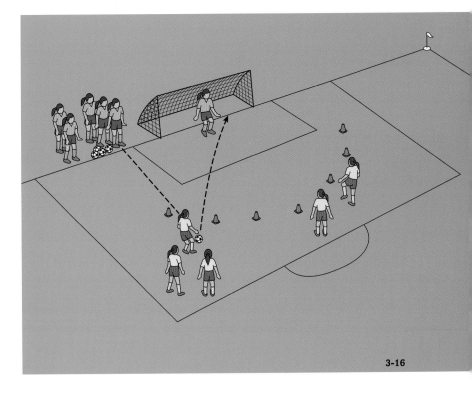

INSTEP DRIVE

ORGANIZATION Nine players plus a goalkeeper, 10 soccer balls, six cones. The coach's position should be alongside the goal with the soccer balls. All of the players, with the exception of the goalkeeper should be stationed outside the "D"-shaped part of the penalty area (3-17). The coach plays a ball into area #1. One player advances forward and tries to score with an instep drive. Following the attempt, the player returns to the top of the "D" as the coach delivers another pass, this time into area #2. The player should try again to score with the instep drive. If unsuccessful with both shots, the player goes behind the goal to assist in retrieving balls. If successful in scoring one attempt, the player may go back to the group and wait another turn. If a player scores twice, the player can nominate a teammate to come forward; the nominated player must score both times or else will also have to help retrieve the balls from behind the goal.

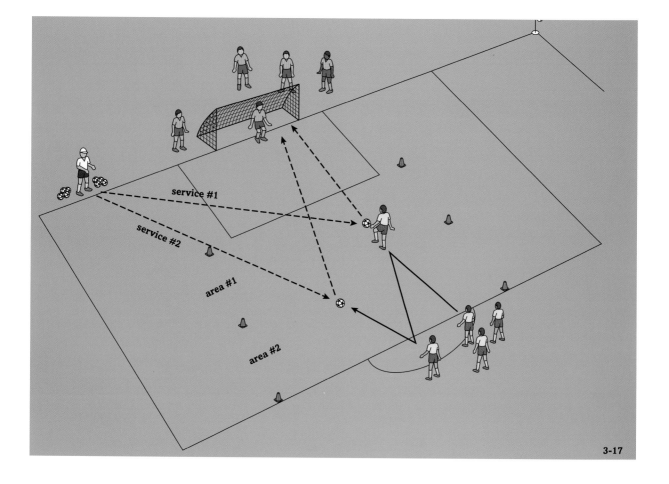

service #1

service #2

area #1

area #2

3-17

GROUND CONTROL

ORGANIZATION 10 players split into two groups of three and one group of four with one soccer ball. The three groups form a triangle 15 yds x 15 yds x 15 yds. The group of four commences the practice with the ball. A player passes the ball and follows the pass to the back of the other line (3-18).

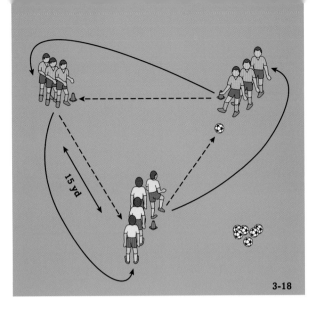

3-18

GROUND CONTROL

FIELD SIZE 10-yd x 10-yd grid.

ORGANIZATION 10 players split into four groups, two of two and two of three, two soccer balls, four cones. The groups of three should commence the practice, passing the ball with the inside of the foot and following the pass. The receiving players should control with the inside of the foot, return the ball, and follow it (3-19). A competitive game can be made by playing the two groups against each other or the two groups against the clock, e.g., completing a predetermined number of passes within a given time frame.

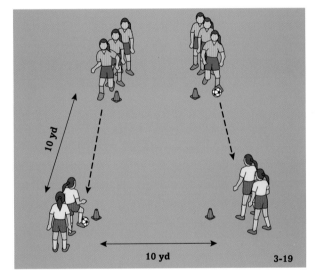

3-19

GROUND CONTROL

ORGANIZATION 10 players, two groups of five, one soccer ball and five cones per group. Place the cones in a zigzag formation approximately 12 yards apart with a player in front of each cone. Each group must pass the ball back and forth in the zigzag formation (3-20). Make a competitive game by playing one group against the other.

3-20

GROUND CONTROL

ORGANIZATION 10 players (two groups of five) form two circles, one ball per circle. Each player will call the name of the intended receiver, pass and follow the ball, then fill the space left by that receiver. The receiver comes and collects the ball and repeats the exercise (3-21).

3-21

AERIAL CONTROL

ORGANIZATION The player throws the ball up in the air and lets the ball bounce (3-22, 3-23). After the bounce, the player can use any of the six controlling surfaces: either foot, either thigh, chest, or head.

3-22 a

3-22 b

3-23 a

3-23b

AERIAL CONTROL

ORGANIZATION 10 players in five pairs, each pair in a 10-yd x 10-yd grid; Five soccer balls, 11 cones. One player throws the ball up in the air. Allowing only one bounce, the other player must use one of the six controlling surfaces to bring the ball under control (3-24). If the ball stays in the grid after the control, that player gets one point. Change roles after a certain number of throws. Then play pair-on-pair.

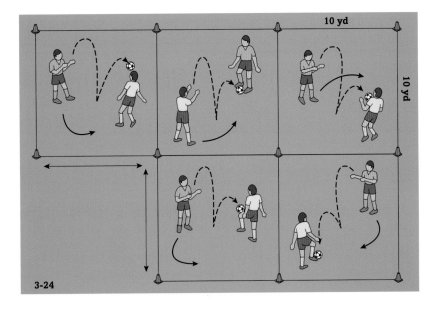

3-24

AERIAL CONTROL

ORGANIZATION 10 players in five pairs, each pair in a 10-yd x 20-yd grid. Five soccer balls, 22 cones. The player with the ball serves it underhand so it will bounce in the partner's half of the grid. This player can use any one of the six controlling surfaces to control the ball after the first bounce. Then, on the second or third touch, the player must play the ball back through the cones to the partner (3-25).

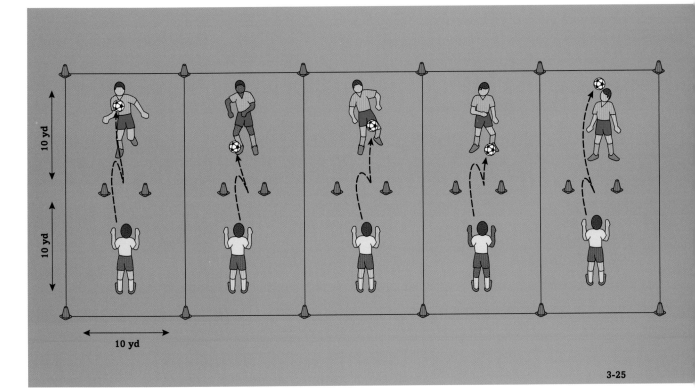

3-25

AERIAL CONTROL

FIELD SIZE 10-yd x 10-yd grid.

ORGANIZATION Players in groups of three, two soccer balls per group. One of the end players serves the ball underhand to a receiving player. The receiver controls using any one of the six controlling surfaces and plays the ball back to the same server. The receiver then turns and controls a ball from another serving player, and repeats the exercise (3-26). After a period of time, change the players around until each has had a turn at receiving. Keep the ball in the grid.

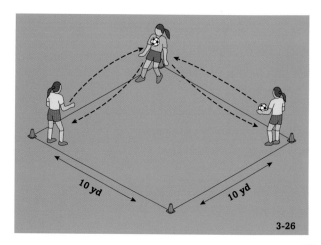

3-26

AERIAL CONTROL

FIELD SIZE 10-yd x 10-yd grid.

ORGANIZATION Players in groups of three, one soccer ball per group. The player with the ball serves underhand to the receiving player. The receiving player then controls and turns, using one of the six controlling surfaces, and plays the ball to the other player, who picks it up and repeats the exercise (3-27).

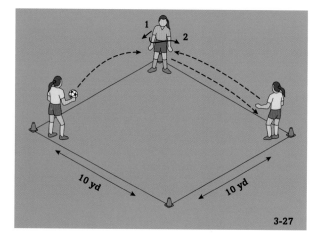

3-27

Coaching Points
- Get in line and underneath the ball.
- Make an early decision on which controlling surface to use.
- Be relaxed on contact.

HEADING *(Individual)*

ORGANIZATION The player throws the soccer ball lightly up into the air and attempts to juggle it on the head (3-28). With this age-group, the coach may want to use a rubber ball or a soft soccer ball to help reduce the fear factor.

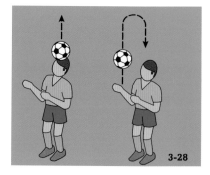

3-28

ORGANIZATION 10 players, in pairs, one soccer ball per pair. The receiving player sits down (3-29, 3-30). The serving player stands a few yards away and serves the ball underhand for the receiver to head back. The sitting player should keep the trunk upright and the neck stiff. The arms are pulled back to increase power in the header. After a certain number of headers, change the players around.

HEADING

ORGANIZATION 10 players, in pairs, one soccer ball per pair. The receiving player kneels down (3-31, 3-32). The serving player stands a few yards away and serves the ball underhand for the receiver to head back. The kneeling player should be tilted backwards, not sitting on the legs, and should rock forward from the hips, keeping the upper torso and neck stiff. The arms are pulled back to increase power in the header.

Coaching Points

- Move forward to meet the ball.
- Arch body and snap forward for maximum power.
- Ensure contact is made with the forehead.
- Eyes should be open and mouth closed.

GOALKEEPING *(Basic Handling, Ground, Stoop Technique)*

ORGANIZATION Goalkeepers in pairs, one soccer ball per pair. Two cones. Goalkeepers standing 10 yards apart facing each other. Each keeper takes a turn at rolling the ball along the ground to the other keeper, who collects it in the stoop technique (3-33).

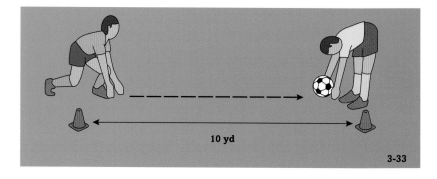

10 yd

3-33

GOALKEEPING *(Basic Handling, Ground, Stoop Technique-Including Footwork)*

ORGANIZATION Goalkeepers in pairs using a number of soccer balls. Goals should be marked by placing cones six yards apart; another cone should be placed 1½ yards inside each post. The goalkeeper should start in the center of the goal for each service. Balls are rolled along the ground to the shaded area (3-34). The goalkeeper should shuffle sideways to collect the ball, using the stoop technique.

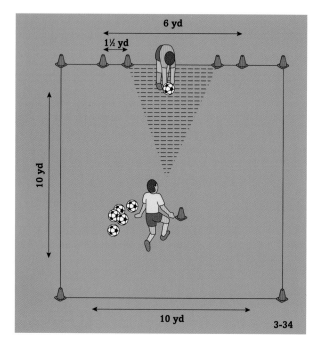

6 yd

1½ yd

10 yd

10 yd

3-34

Coaching Points

- Head steady and eyes on the ball
- Get in line with the ball
- Ensure short sideways strides as goalkeeper adjusts
- Hands positioned behind the ball
- Feet behind the ball and close together
- Bend from the waist; do not squat
- Cup ball to the chest

GOALKEEPING *(Basic handling, Ground, Stoop Technique—Including Footwork)*

ORGANIZATION Goalkeepers in pairs using a number of soccer balls. Goals should be set up using cones placed six yards apart; another cone should be placed two yards inside each post. A ball should be rolled along the ground to the shaded area (3-35). The goalkeeper should collect the ball in the stoop technique.

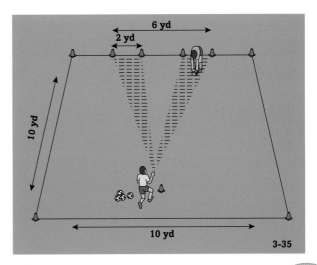

3-35

GOALKEEPING *(Distribution, Kicking—Dead Ball)*

ORGANIZATION Goalkeepers in pairs, one soccer ball per pair. Goalkeepers spaced 20 yards apart. The ball should be kicked from the ground; the partner collects it and returns it in the same manner (3-36).

Coaching Points
• Same as for a lofted pass.

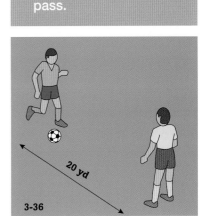

3-36

GOALKEEPING *(Distribution, Kicking—Volley)*

ORGANIZATION Goalkeepers in pairs, one soccer ball per pair. Goalkeepers spaced 20 yards apart. The ball should be dropped from the hands and kicked; the partner collects it and returns it in the same manner (3-37).

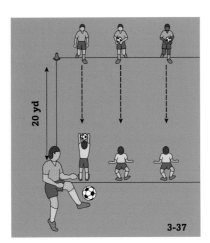

3-37

Coaching Points
• Approach the ball straight on.
• Hold and drop the ball from both hands.
• Head down with eyes on the ball.
• Lean slightly back on contact.
• The ball makes contact with the lace part of the shoe, and the toe should be pointed away.

GOALKEEPING *(Distribution, Kicking—Half Volley)*

ORGANIZATION Goalkeepers in pairs, one soccer ball per pair. Goalkeepers spaced 20 yards apart. The ball should be dropped from both hands and half-volleyed to the partner, who collects it and returns it in the same manner (3-38).

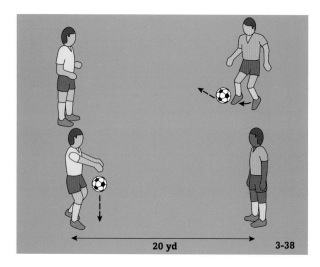

20 yd — 3-38

Coaching Points

- Approach the ball straight on.
- Hold and drop the ball from both hands.
- Head down with eyes on the ball.
- Lean slightly back on contact.
- The kicking foot makes contact with the ball as it strikes the ground.
- The ball makes contact with the laces of the shoe.
- Ankle locked and toe pointed down.

GOALKEEPING *(Shot Stopping—Ground)*

ORGANIZATION Goalkeepers in pairs, one soccer ball per pair. Goalkeepers spaced three yards apart. One goalkeeper kneels. The other goalkeeper hand-serves the ball by rolling it to the left of the kneeling player, who dives to stop it (3-39). The ball should be returned and the exercise repeated to the right side of the kneeling player. After repeating the exercise six times on each side, the players should reverse positions.

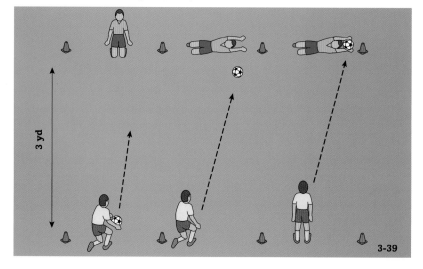

3 yd — 3-39

Coaching Points

- Head steady, eyes fixed on the ball.
- One hand behind the ball and the other on top of it.
- Keeper should land on side, not on stomach.
- Pull the ball in towards the body to complete the save.

GOALKEEPING *(Shot Stopping-Air)*

ORGANIZATION Goalkeepers in pairs, one soccer ball per pair. Goalkeepers spaced three yards apart. One goalkeeper kneels. The other goalkeeper hand-serves the ball by throwing it in the air to the left side of the kneeling player, who dives to stop it (3-40). The ball should be returned and the exercise repeated to the right side of the kneeling player. After repeating the exercise six times on each side, the players should reverse positions.

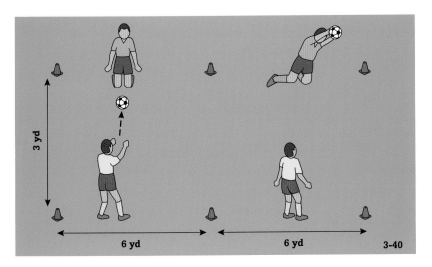

3 yd

6 yd   6 yd   3-40

GOALKEEPING *(Shot Stopping—Air)*

ORGANIZATION Goalkeepers in pairs, one soccer ball per pair. Goalkeepers spaced three yards apart. One goalkeeper squats. The other goalkeeper hand-serves the ball by throwing it in the air to the left side of the squatting player, who springs sideways to make the save (3-41). The ball should be returned and the exercise repeated to the right side of the squatting player. After repeating the exercise six times on each side, the players should reverse positions.

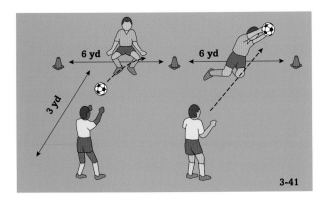

6 yd   6 yd

3 yd

3-41

Team Games

Understanding the game is the most important aspect of a player's development. If a player understands why depth or width is important in a small-sided game, the player should be able to adapt freely in a full game.

The principles of play can provide the foundation upon which the future development of positional play can take place. Therefore, they should be used as a framework on which all teaching and coaching is developed.

ATTACK

PENETRATION Moving the ball into or through the opposition defense.

WIDTH Playing the balls into wide positions to draw defenders away from each other.

DEPTH Allowing the player to pass the ball through 360 degrees.

SUPPORT Supporting the teammate on the ball

COMMUNICATION Providing the player receiving the ball with verbal support so the player has direction (hold, turn, etc.).

MOBILITY The movement of players in front or behind the player with the ball affecting the position of defensive players.

IMPROVISATION Players changing roles or doing the unusual.

DEFENSE

PRESSURE ON THE BALL Blocking the opponent's way towards goal. Channeling the attacker into nonscoring areas.

DELAY Jockeying to allow other defenders time to cover.

DEPTH Covering the pressuring player and the space behind.

BALANCE Covering the supporting player and the space behind.

CONCENTRATION Keeping your attention and focus on the play.

COMMUNICATION The supporting player must give verbal instruction to the pressuring player.

CONTROL & RESTRAINT Defenders not selling themselves in the tackle, i.e., committing to the tackle too early or being too far away from the opponent to be effective, thereby causing effecting delay.

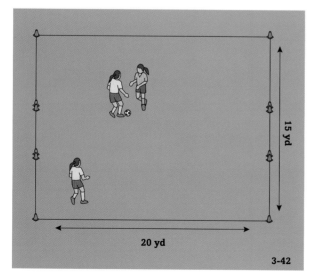

15 yd

20 yd

3-42

FIELD SIZE 20 yds x 15 yds.

ORGANIZATION Two-on-one (3-42).

For all team games, when the ball goes out of play, restart from the touch line with a kick in. When the ball goes out over the goal line, the game is always restarted by a goal kick.

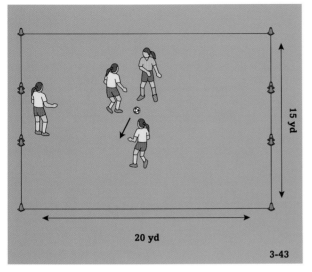

3-43

FIELD SIZE 20 yds x 15 yds.

ORGANIZATION Two-on-one plus a goalkeeper (3-43).

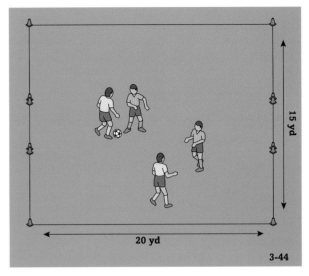

3-44

FIELD SIZE 20 yds x 15 yds.

ORGANIZATION Two-on-two (3-44).

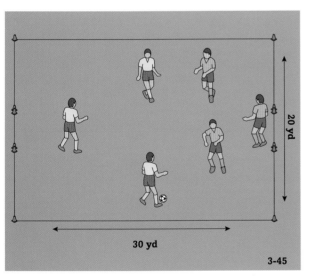

3-45

FIELD SIZE 30 yds x 20 yds.

ORGANIZATION Three-on-two plus a goalkeeper (3-45).

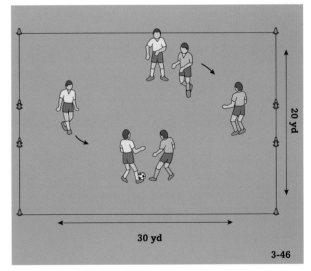

3-46

FIELD SIZE 30 yds x 20 yds.

ORGANIZATION Three-on-three (3-46).

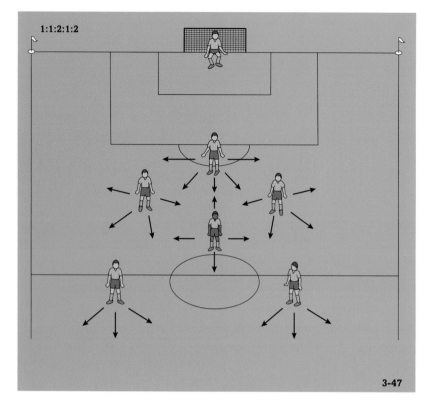

1:1:2:1:2

3-47

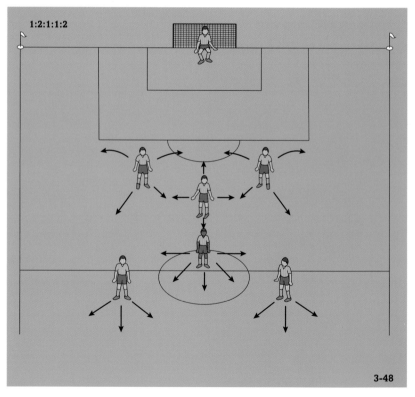

1:2:1:1:2

3-48

Chapter 4

U-10 Drills & Practices

(under age 10)

*A*t this age level, continue to concentrate team play on small-sided games. Place your emphasis on skill development while encouraging players to spread out.

Length of Training Session:
55-65 MINUTES

Warm-up 10 minutes
Technique/Skill
Development 20 minutes
Team Game 10-15 minutes
Free Play 15-20 minutes

Practices

WARM-UP

FIELD SIZE 10-yd x 10-yd grids.

ORGANIZATION 12 players in four groups of three, four soccer balls, 10 cones. The players should pass and move inside their grid using no more than two touches and all foot surfaces to control the ball (4-1).

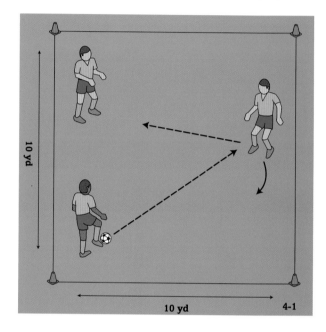

10 yd

10 yd

4-1

SHIELDING

FIELD SIZE 20-yd x 20-yd grid.

ORGANIZATION 12 players, nine with a soccer ball. The players without a ball try to kick the soccer ball out from the other players' control (4-2). This should be done within a time limit.

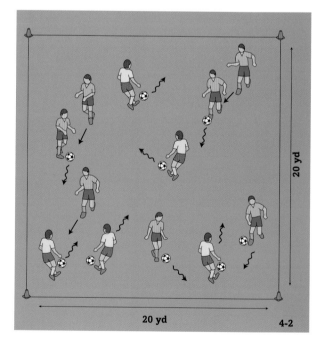

20 yd

20 yd

4-2

SHIELDING

FIELD SIZE 30-yd x 30-yd grid.

ORGANIZATION Players in pairs, one soccer ball per pair, four cones. The player in possession of the ball shields it while the other player tries to win it (4-3). When this is accomplished, the ball is returned. After a time period, the roles are reversed. Count the times each player wins the ball.

Coaching Points

- Do not show the ball.
- Keep the ball on the farthest foot.
- Make a long barrier with your body.

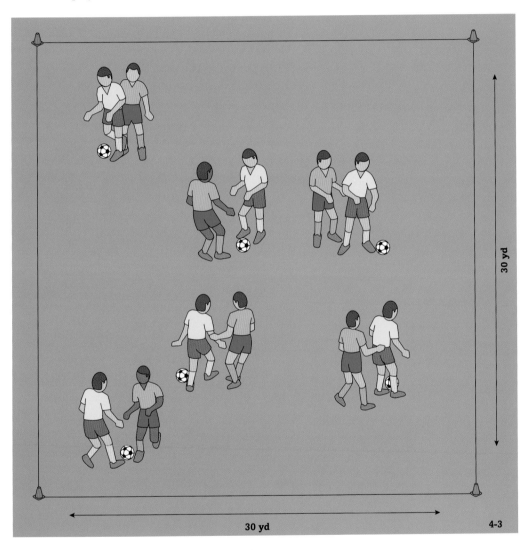

30 yd

30 yd

4-3

MOVES—TURNS

FIELD SIZE Two 10-yd x 10-yd grids.

ORGANIZATION 12 players, each with a soccer ball, six cones. Each player dribbles a ball around inside the whole grid area (4-4). The coach nominates a grid that the players sprint into with their ball. They continue dribbling there until they receive another command to sprint as before.

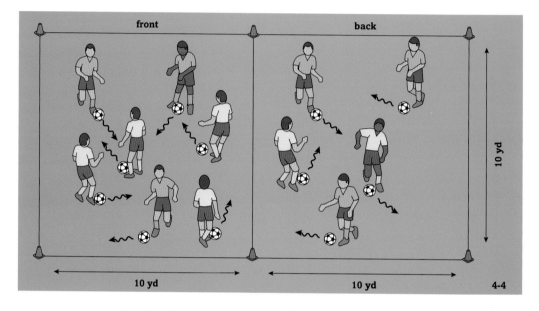

MOVES—TURNS

FIELD SIZE Two 10-yd x 10-yd grids.

ORGANIZATION Players in pairs with one soccer ball per pair, six cones. The player with the ball attempts to dribble and carry it over the end line of the grid (4-5). Encourage the attacking player to use different tricks to beat the opponent. After five attempts per player, have them change roles.

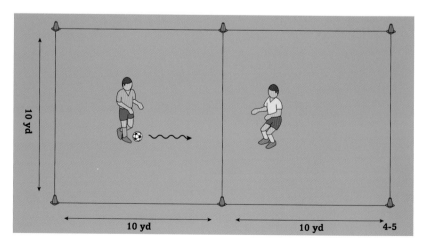

MOVES—TURNS

FIELD SIZE 30 yds. long

ORGANIZATION 12 players, four groups of three, one soccer ball per group, eight cones. A player on the outside plays the ball to the player in the middle (4-6). The player in the middle comes to meet the ball, then glances over the shoulder before turning with the ball and playing it to the player at the opposite end. Repeat the exercise and encourage players to use different surfaces.

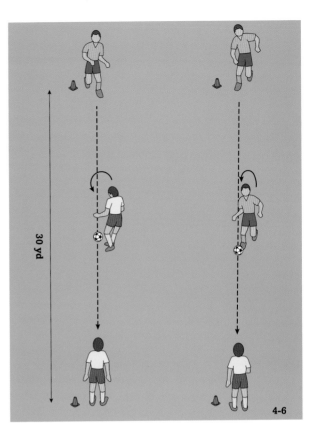

MOVES—TURNS

FIELD SIZE Four 20-yd x 10-yd grids.

ORGANIZATION 12 players, four groups of three, one soccer ball per group, 15 cones. The ball is served to the player in the middle of the grid; this player comes to meet it, then glances over the shoulder before turning quickly, attempting to beat the defender while dribbling the ball over the end line (4-7). Repeat the exercise and encourage players to use different turning surfaces and tricks.

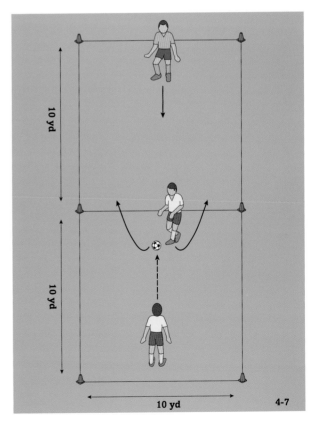

KICKING WITH THE INSIDE OF THE FOOT

FIELD SIZE 20-yd x 20-yd grid.

ORGANIZATION 12 players, four groups of three, one soccer ball, four cones. One player passes the ball and follows it to any one of the other three groups (4-8). Each player should be limited to two touches before passing.

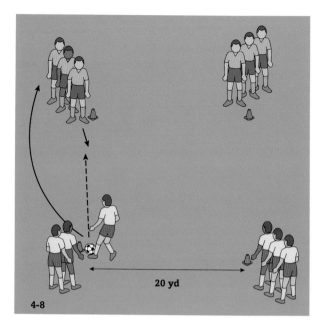

KICKING WITH THE INSIDE OF THE FOOT

FIELD SIZE 10-yd x 10-yd grids.

ORGANIZATION 12 players in pairs, one soccer ball per pair; 12 cones. To commence the practice, one player passes the ball to the other, who controls and takes it around the cone before passing it back, attempting to knock over the partner's cone (4-9).

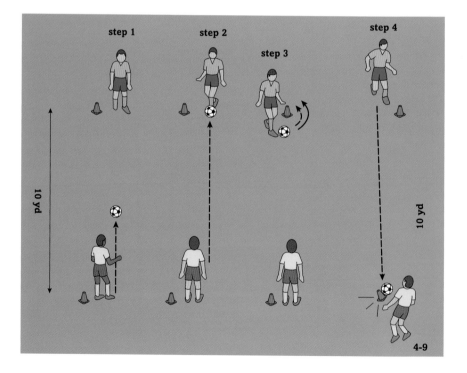

KICKING WITH THE INSIDE OF THE FOOT

FIELD SIZE 10-yd x 10-yd grids.

ORGANIZATION Players in groups of five, one soccer ball and four cones per group. Four players are restricted to their side of the grid and must not enter inside. The player in the middle cannot leave the grid (4-10). The object is to pass the ball from the outside diagonally or straight across the grid without the defender intercepting the ball. Should one of the outside players make a mistake, such as a bad pass or poor control, then that player switches places with the defender.

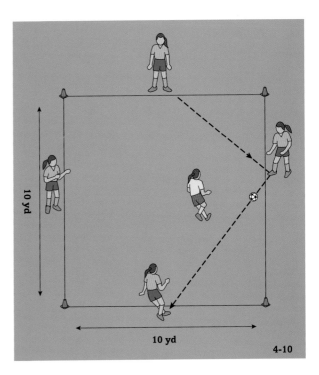

INSTEP KICKING

FIELD SIZE Six 20-yd x 10-yd grids.

ORGANIZATION 12 players in pairs, one soccer ball per group, 14 cones. The ball should be passed between partners using the instep. On receiving, the player controls the ball to the side, then passes it back to the partner who repeats the exercise (4-11). Encourage players to use either foot.

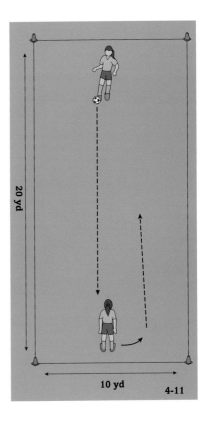

FIELD SIZE Four 40-yd x 10-yd grids.

ORGANIZATION 12 players in groups of three, one soccer ball per group, 18 cones. To commence the practice a ball is rolled out by the goalkeeper (4-12). The kicker tries to score with an instep drive. If the ball is saved, the goalkeeper turns and rolls it to the player on the opposite side. If the kicker scores or the ball goes past, the goalkeeper must recover and anticipate a shot from the player on the opposite side. Keep score and change roles.

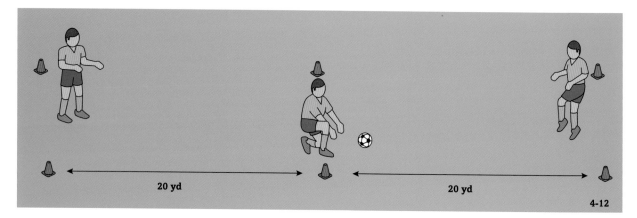

20 yd   20 yd

4-12

FIELD SIZE 25-yd x 25-yd grid.

ORGANIZATION 12 players in groups of two, one soccer ball per group, seven cones. Partners stand on opposite sides of the grid facing each other, with the object being to knock over the cones in the middle of the grid using an instep drive (4-13).

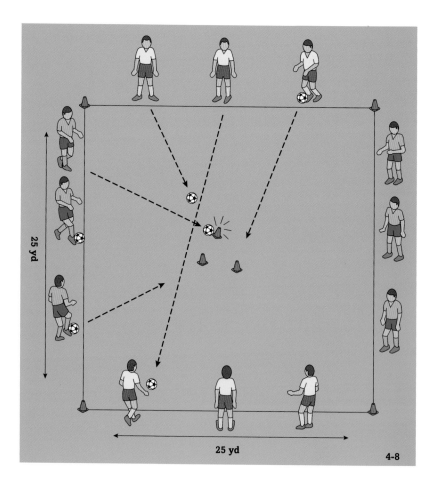

25 yd

25 yd

4-8

KICKING WITH THE OUTSIDE OF THE FOOT

FIELD SIZE 20-yd x 20-yd grid.

ORGANIZATION 12 players, eight balls, four cones. Eight players, each with a soccer ball, stand outside the grid facing the four players on the inside of the grid. The players with the ball strike it with the outside of the foot and try to hit the players in the middle below the waist (4-14). The kicking player retrieves the ball.

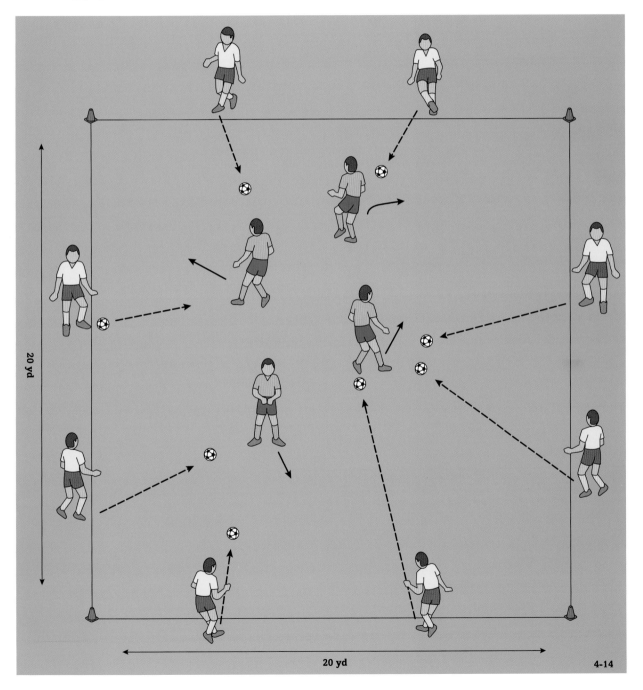

20 yd

20 yd

4-14

FIELD SIZE 20-yd x 20-yd grid.

ORGANIZATION 12 players, four groups of three, one soccer ball, four cones. Each group is stationed at a cone. The player with the ball passes it with the outside of the foot to the first player in any one of the other groups, and follows the pass (4-15).

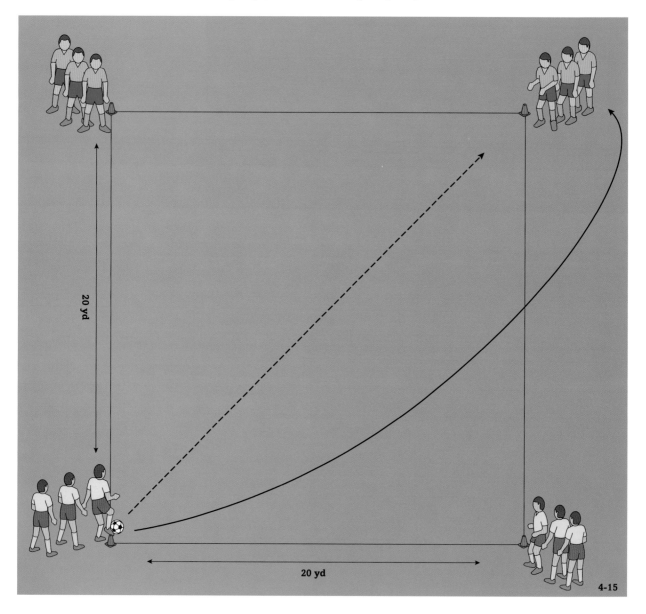

20 yd

20 yd

4-15

KICKING WITH THE OUTSIDE OF THE FOOT

FIELD SIZE 30-yd x 40-yd grid.

ORGANIZATION 12 players in pairs, six soccer balls, four cones. Each pair moves around inside the whole area of the grid, passing the ball to each other using the outside of the foot (4-16). Encourage players to pass with either foot.

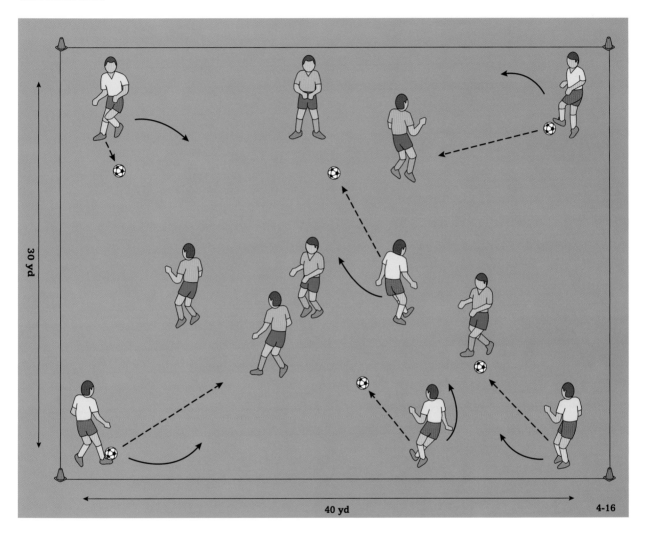

30 yd

40 yd

4-16

FIELD SIZE 20-yd x 20-yd grid.

ORGANIZATION 12 players in pairs, six soccer balls. The player on the outside passes the ball to a partner in the inside circle. This player controls and returns it before turning left to receive another pass (4-17).

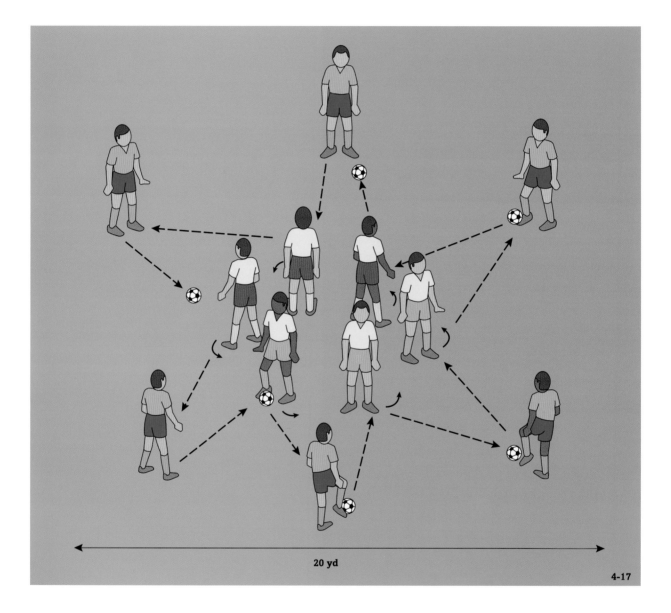

20 yd

4-17

GROUND CONTROL

FIELD SIZE 20-yd x 20-yd grid.

ORGANIZATION 12 players in groups of three, one soccer ball, four cones. Each player passes the ball diagonally in a clockwise direction and follows the pass to the back of the group (4-18). Each pass should be controlled with the left foot and passed with the right foot. Then have players work the practice counterclockwise, reversing the use of the feet.

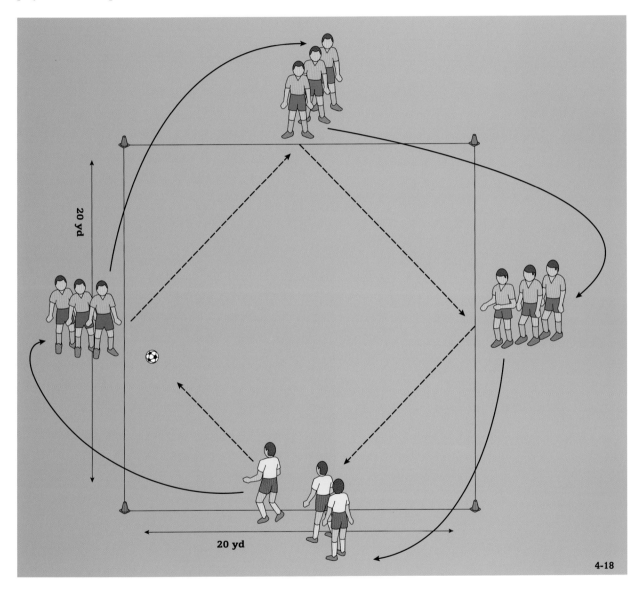

20 yd

20 yd

4-18

FIELD SIZE 10-yd x 10-yd grid.

ORGANIZATION 12 players in groups of three, two soccer balls, four cones. The first players of each group pass the ball to the first player on the group opposite (4-19). The player follows the pass through to the end of that group. Using no more than two touches to control the ball, the pass is returned. During this practice, players try not to hit the other group's ball.

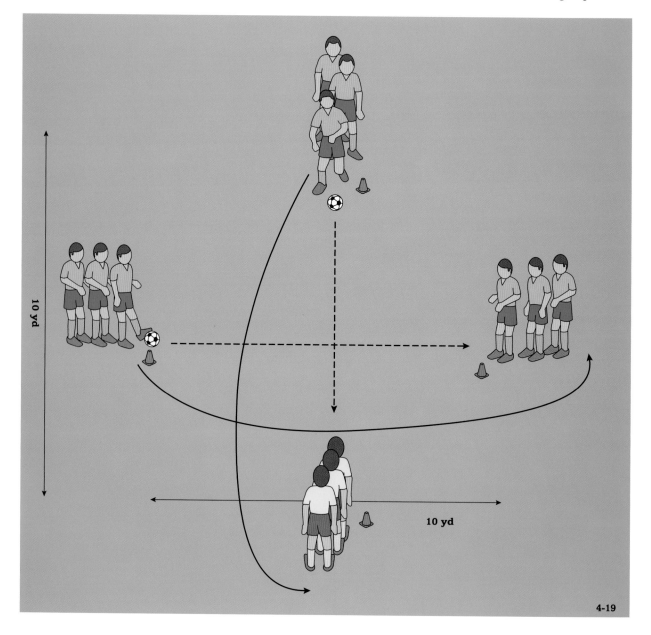

10 yd

10 yd

4-19

AERIAL CONTROL

ORGANIZATION 12 players in pairs, six soccer balls, 10 cones. Place players eight yards apart. The player with the ball delivers it using a proper throw-in (4-20). The receiving player must control the ball with the surface designated by the coach and then pass it back. This practice can be developed so that when the ball is played back, the thrower has to control and catch it.

AERIAL CONTROL

ORGANIZATION 12 players in pairs, six soccer balls, 10 cones. Place players five yards apart. The first player with the ball delivers it underhand (4-21). The receiving player must control it with a surface designated by the coach, let it bounce, then pass it back.

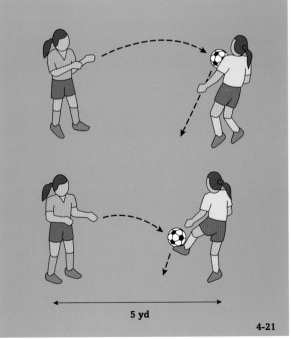

step 1

step 2

step 3

5 yd

4-22

ORGANIZATION 12 players in pairs, six soccer balls, 10 cones. Place players five yards apart. The player with the ball delivers it underhand; the receiving player must control it with a surface designated by the coach, let it bounce, then pass it back (4-22). The first player must now control the ball with a surface designated by the coach and catch it for a point.

HEADING

FIELD SIZE Six 10-yd x 10-yd grids.

ORGANIZATION 12 players in pairs, one soccer ball per pair, 12 cones. One pair per grid. To start the practice, one player throws the ball in the air and attempts to score a goal by heading it past a partner (4-23). Alternate turns.

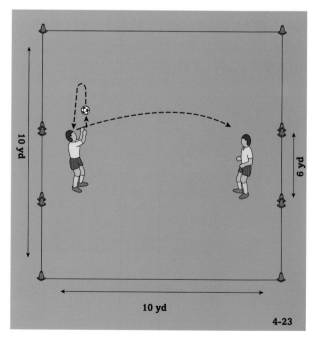

10 yd

10 yd

6 yd

4-23

HEADING

FIELD SIZE 10-yd x 10-yd grids.

ORGANIZATION 12 players in pairs, one soccer ball
per pair, 12 cones per grid. One pair per grid. To start
the practice, the player with the ball throws it
underhand to a partner who attempts to score a goal
by heading it back past the serving player (4-24).
Players alternate turns.

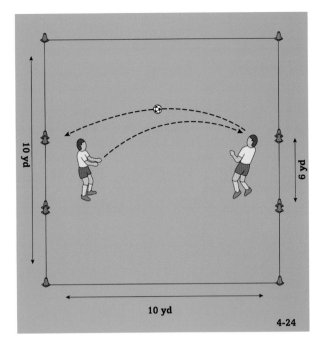

4-24

HEADING

ORGANIZATION 12 players in two groups of six.
One player from each group stands by a goalpost; the
other five members of the group stand 15 yards from
goal. The player at the goalpost serves the ball so it will
bounce; after the bounce, the receiving player runs in
and heads the ball into the goal (4-25). To score, the
ball must hit the goal net on the full (fly). After each
attempt the player returns the ball to the server and
goes to the back of the line. After the introduction of
this practice, play the groups against each other.

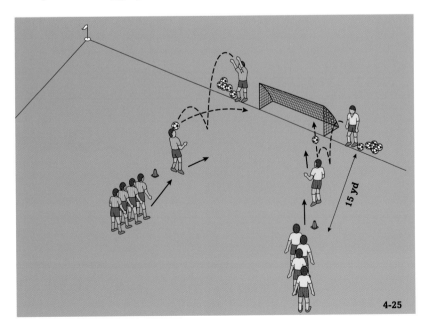

4-25

TACKLING

FIELD SIZE 10-yd x 10-yd grid.

ORGANIZATION 12 players in groups of four, one soccer ball per group. The four players in each group form a square and place themselves facing a partner. One set of partners jog out simultaneously and tackle for the ball in the middle of the grid (4-26). After the tackle they jog back. The exercise is repeated by the other two players in the group.

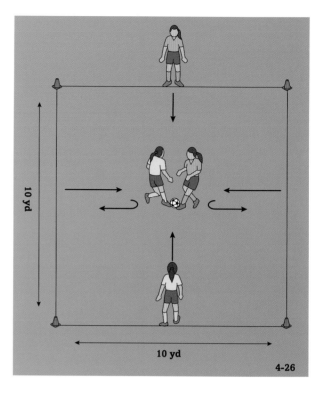

TACKLING

FIELD SIZE 10-yd x 10-yd grid.

ORGANIZATION 12 players in groups of four, two soccer balls per group. The four players in each group form a square and place themselves facing a partner with one ball between each pair. One player dribbles the ball out into the center of the grid, where the partner tackles for it (4-27). After the tackle, both players return to their original positions on the grid and reverse roles. In this exercise the dribbling player does not try to dribble past the tackling player.

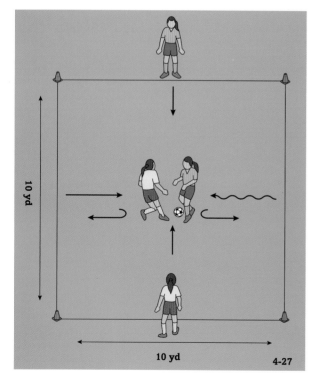

FIELD SIZE 20-yd x 20-yd grid.

ORGANIZATION 12 players, 11 soccer balls, four cones. 11 players, each with a ball, dribble around inside the grid; the 12th player attempts to tackle and kick the balls out of the grid (4-28).

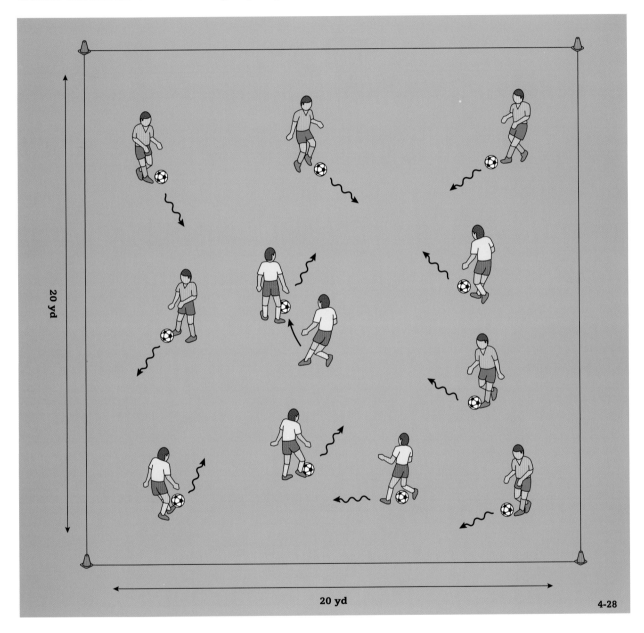

20 yd

20 yd

4-28

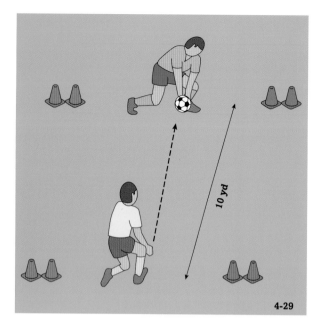

ORGANIZATION Goalkeepers in pairs, with one soccer ball per pair. Place goalkeepers ten yards apart facing each other. Each goalkeeper takes a turn at rolling the ball along the ground one yard to the side of the opposite goalkeeper; the receiver collects it in the kneeling technique and returns the ball in the same manner, alternating the sides the ball is rolled to (4-29).

GOALKEEPING (Basic Handling—Ground Kneeling Technique, Including Footwork)

ORGANIZATION Goalkeepers in pairs, with one soccer ball per pair. Cones are set eight yards apart, forming goals, with another two cones positioned 1½ yards inside each post. The goalkeeper should be positioned in the center of the goal before each service. The server stands ten yards away from the goal and rolls the ball alternately to the left and right of the goalkeeper, aiming for the cones positioned inside each post (4-30). Goalkeepers must shuttle across to receive the ball using the kneeling technique.

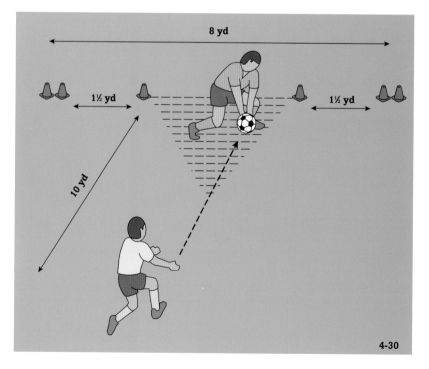

GOALKEEPING
(Basic Handling—Ground Kneeling Technique, Including Footwork)

ORGANIZATION Goalkeepers in pairs, with one soccer ball per pair. Cones are set eight yards apart, forming goals, with another two cones positioned 1½ yards inside each post. The server rolls the ball in between the cones and the post (4-31). Encourage the goalkeeper to shuttle across and collect the ball with the kneeling technique.

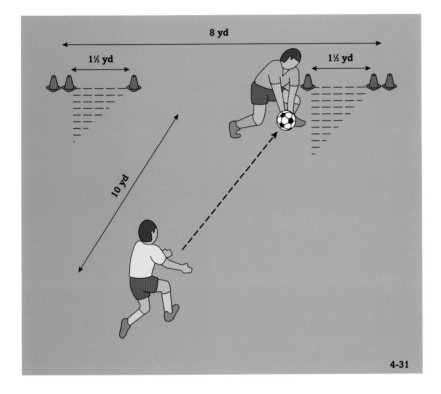

4-31

GOALKEEPING (Basic Handling—Waist Shots)

FIELD SIZE 6-yd x 8-yd grid.

ORGANIZATION Goalkeepers in pairs, one soccer ball per pair. Both goalkeepers kneel facing each other. In turn, each goalkeeper throws the ball underhand towards the waist of the partner (4-32). Encourage the goalkeepers to reach forward and collect the ball early. If the ball is played to the side, the goalkeeper should cup the ball to the body and land on the shoulder—not the elbow.

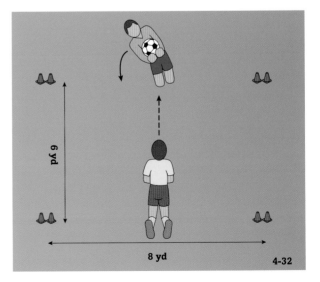

4-32

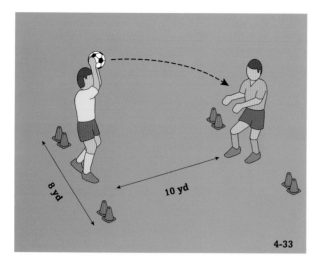

GOALKEEPING *(Basic Handling—Chest Shots)*

FIELD SIZE 8-yd x 10-yd grid.

ORGANIZATION Goalkeepers in pairs, one soccer ball per pair. In turn, each goalkeeper throws the ball overarm towards the chest area of the partner (4-33). Encourage the goalkeeper to step and/or reach forward to collect the ball early. If the ball has been played to the side, the goalkeeper should move sideways and ensure that the body and the arms are behind the ball.

GOALKEEPING *(Basic Handling—Waist and Chest Shots)*

ORGANIZATION Goalkeepers in pairs, with a number of soccer balls; two cones. Balls are kicked waist- or chest-high to the goalkeeper in the center area of the goal (4-34). Once the goalkeeper shows good technique, the balls should be served towards the cones placed two yards inside each goal post. Encourage the correct sideways movement from the goalkeeper. Goalkeepers change positions every 20 shots.

Coaching Points

- Head steady and eyes on the ball.
- Ensure body and arms are behind the ball on contact.
- Cup the ball into the body for protection.
- If it is necessary to dive, land on the shoulder— not on the elbow.

GOALKEEPING *(Distribution—Underarm Throw)*

ORGANIZATION Goalkeepers in pairs with a number of soccer balls, four cones. Goalkeeper receives a ball played in by the server and rolls it underarm through either of the two pairs of cones placed two yards apart and positioned five yards outside each corner of the penalty area (4-35). Goalkeepers change positions after 20 throws.

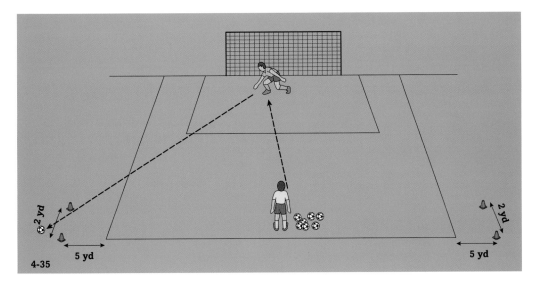

GOALKEEPING *(Distribution—Javelin Throw)*

ORGANIZATION Goalkeepers in pairs with a supply of soccer balls, four cones. The goalkeeper in the goal area receives a ball from the server and throws it javelin style through either pair of two cones spaced four yards apart and positioned ten yards from each corner of the penalty area (4-36). The goalkeeper should throw from inside the six-yard box. The ball may bounce before passing through the cones. Insist on accuracy. Goalkeepers change positions every 20 throws.

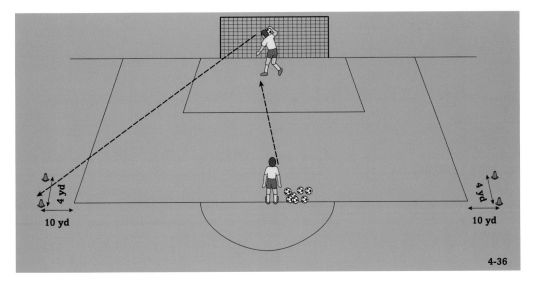

GOALKEEPING
(Distribution—Overarm Throw)

ORGANIZATION Goalkeepers in pairs with a supply of soccer balls, four cones. The goalkeeper receives the ball from the server and, from the edge of the penalty area, throws it overarm through two cones placed 10 yards apart, positioned 15 yards from the edge of the penalty area (4-37). Goalkeepers change position every 20 throws.

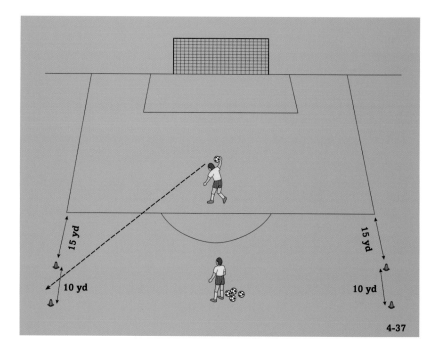

4-37

GOALKEEPING (Shot Stopping—Ground)

ORGANIZATION Goalkeepers in pairs, one soccer ball per pair, six cones. The goalkeeper stands one to two yards behind the goal line and does a forward roll as the ball is served along the ground one yard to the side, forcing the goalkeeper to dive and save (4-38). The exercise should be repeated on alternate sides. Roles should be reversed every 20 saves.

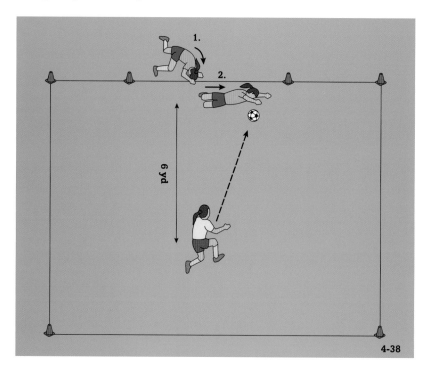

4-38

GOALKEEPING
(Shot Stopping—Air)

ORGANIZATION Goalkeepers in pairs, one soccer ball per pair; six cones. The goalkeeper stands one to two yards behind the goal line. The server stands six yards out in front of the goal with the ball. The goalkeeper does a forward roll as the server throws the ball underarm in the air for the goalkeeper to dive and save (4-39). Roles are reversed every 20 saves.

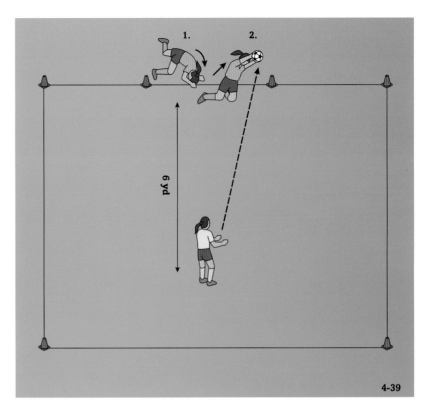

6 yd

4-39

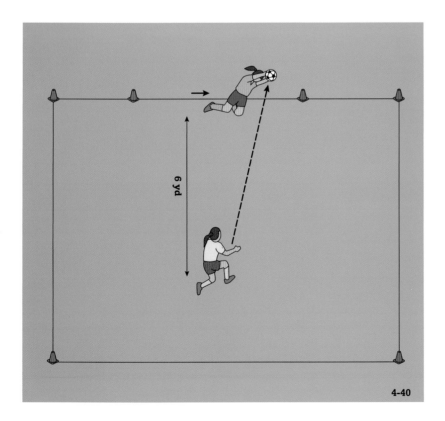

6 yd

4-40

GOALKEEPING
(Shot Stopping—Ground and Air)

ORGANIZATION Goalkeepers in pairs, six soccer balls, six cones. The goalkeeper stands in the goal. The server rolls the ball along the ground or throws it in the air to the goalkeeper's left (4-40). The goalkeeper dives to save it, recovers and returns it to the server, who repeats the exercise to the goalkeeper's right. Reverse roles every 20 saves.

Team Games

For all team games: if the ball goes out of play, restart the game with a goal kick or throw-in.

FIELD SIZE 30 yds x 20 yds.

ORGANIZATION Three-on-three (4-41). Use cones to make small goals two yards wide.

ATTACKING	DEFENDING
Depth	Pressure
Width	Cover
Penetration	Balance
1-2s (wall passes)	
Support	

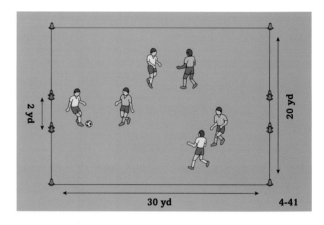

FIELD SIZE 30 yds x 20 yds.

ORGANIZATION Four-on-four (4-42). Use cones to make small goals two yards wide.

ATTACKING	DEFENDING
Depth	Pressure
Width	Cover
Penetration	Balance
1-2s (wall passes)	
Support	

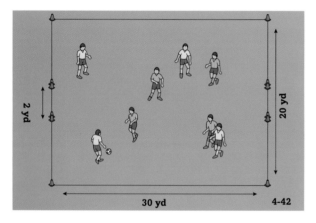

FIELD SIZE 30 yds x 20 yds.

ORGANIZATION Four-on-three plus a goalkeeper (4-43). Use cones to make small goals six yards wide. The nearest defending player to the goal must retreat and become the goalkeeper until possession has been won.

ATTACKING	DEFENDING
Depth	Delay
Width	Pressure
Penetration	Cover
1-2s (wall passes)	Balance
Support	

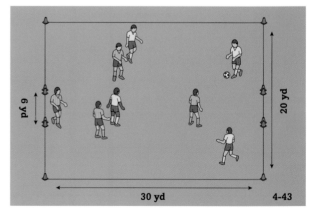

FIELD SIZE 20-yd x 20-yd grid.

ORGANIZATION Three-on-three, four cones (4-44). Three teams of three. Two teams play against each other. To score a goal, a team must knock over a cone with the ball. The teams can play either inside or outside of the cones. The team that scores goes off and the third team comes on.

ATTACKING	DEFENDING
Depth	Pressure
Width	Cover
Penetration	Balance
Changing point of attack	
1-2s (wall passes), Support	

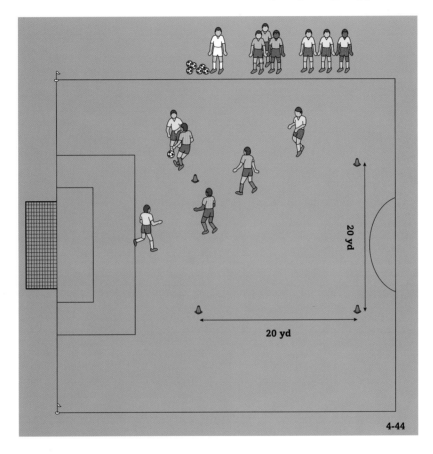

4-44

ORGANIZATION Three teams of three (4-45). Two teams play three-on-three with a central goal. Both teams can score from either side of the goal. The team that scores goes off, and the third team comes on.

ATTACKING	DEFENDING
Depth	Pressure
Width	Cover
Penetration	

4-45

ORGANIZATION One of the most asked questions is, how do you get a young team to spread out and recognize space. There is no easy answer, but the series of practices that follows will help. Divide the field into thirds vertically.

THREE-ON-ZERO. No pressure (4-46). During the course of each practice, the attacking players cannot leave their third. The practice starts when the player in the middle third passes the ball into either of the outside thirds. The players continue passing and moving down the field, finishing with a shot on goal. When the shot on goal is complete, the next group repeats the exercise.

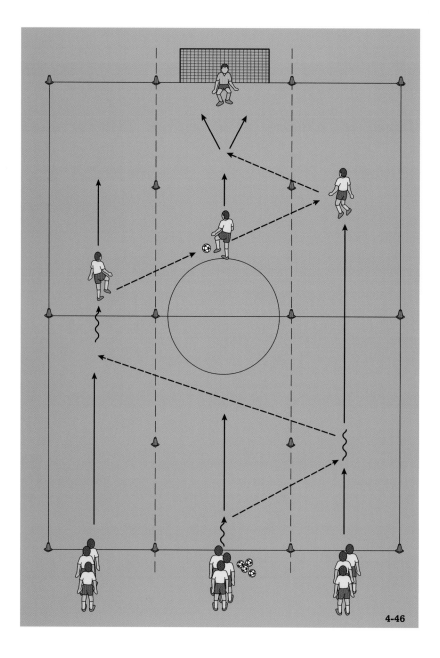

4-46

THREE-ON-ONE. Increase pressure (4-47). Add a defender to provide pressure. The defender is free to move from third to third.

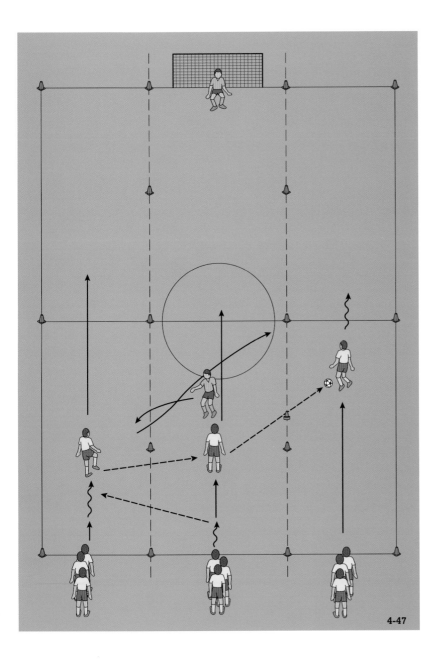

4-47

THREE-ON-TWO. Further increase of pressure (4-48). Increase the pressure by adding a second defender; same freedom applies.

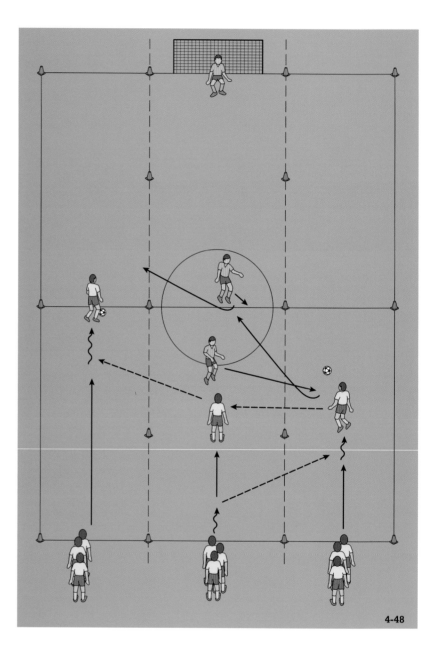

4-48

Two other methods of getting players to spread out and support are:

FIVE-ON-ONE. Play five attackers against one defender (4-49). Same restrictions and freedoms apply.

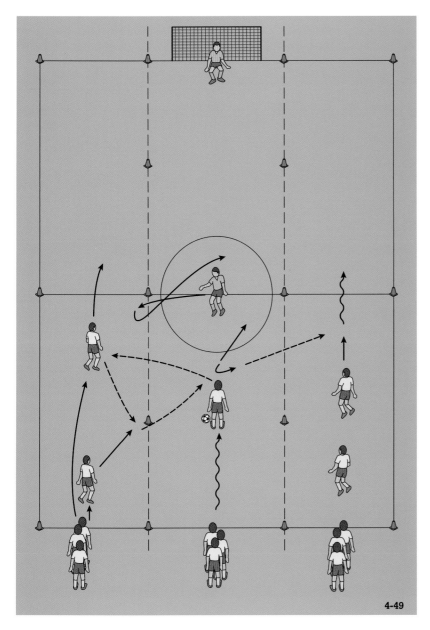

4-49

FIVE-ON-TWO. Increase pressure (4-50). Increase the pressure by adding a second defender; same freedom applies.

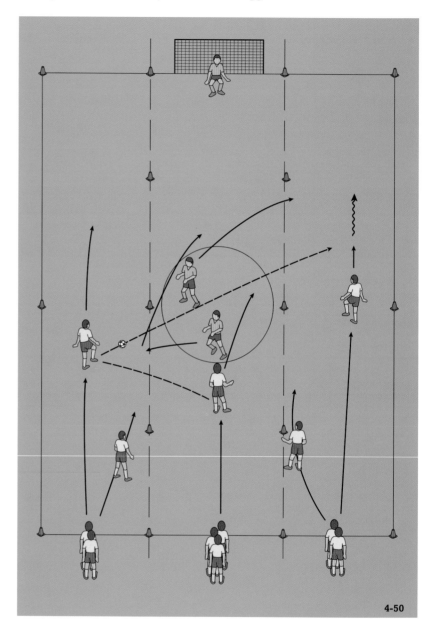

4-50

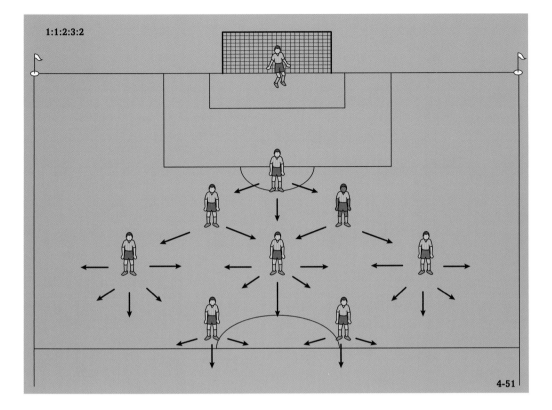

1:1:2:3:2

4-51

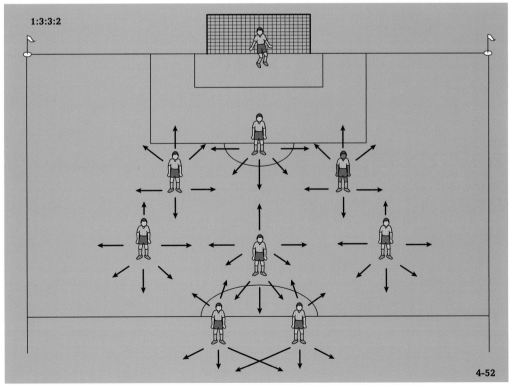

1:3:3:2

4-52

1:2:4:2

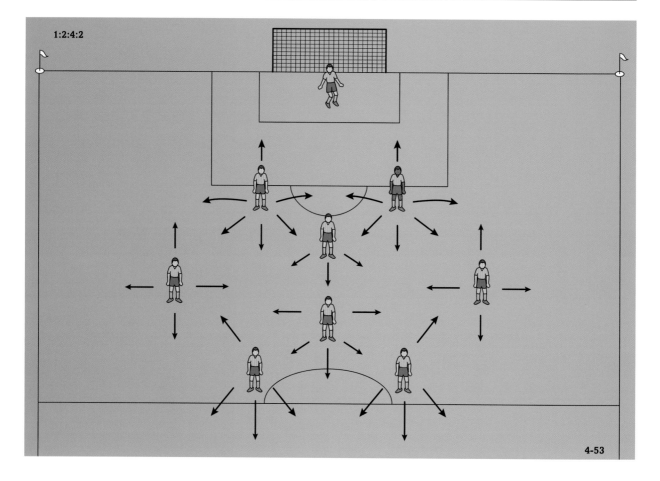

4-53

Chapter 5

U-12 Drills & Practices

(under age 12)

*A*t this age level, small-sided games are still your primary focus for team play, but you also want to concentrate on individual ballwork, juggling, running with the ball, etc. Instruct your players to work in twos and threes, stressing that the emphasis of the exercise is cooperation.

Length of Training Session:
90 MINUTES

Warm-up 10 minutes
Technique/Skill
Development 20 minutes
Team Games/Set Plays
40 minutes
Free Play 20 minutes

Practices

WARM-UP

ORGANIZATION Players in groups of five. The players move around the whole time while playing the ball, performing 1-2s (wall passes) and takeovers (crossover runs) (5-1). Make sure the players use the whole of the area.

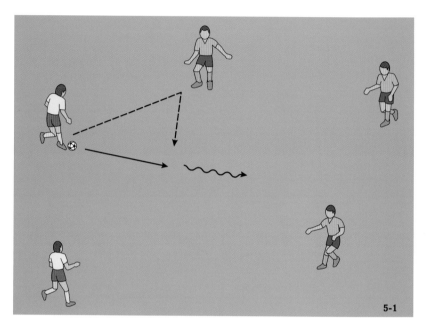

5-1

WARM-UP

FIELD SIZE 20-yd x 20-yd grid.

ORGANIZATION Five-on-two, one soccer ball, four cones. Play five-on-two in the whole of the grid area for two minutes, then change defenders (5-2).

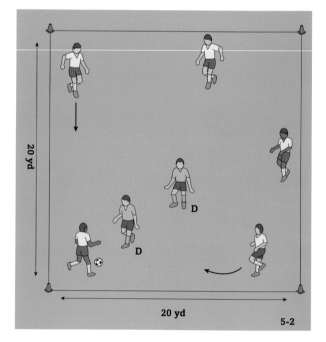

20 yd

20 yd

5-2

WARM-UP

FIELD SIZE Half a field.

ORGANIZATION Players in groups of five, one soccer ball per group. Using the instep, the player with the ball plays it to the farthest player in the group. This player lays it off to one of the supporting players (5-3). The receiving player controls, dribbles, and repeats the exercise.

5-3

DRIBBLING–SHIELDING

FIELD SIZE 20-yd x 10-yd grid.

ORGANIZATION Players in pairs, one soccer ball per pair, six cones. The player with the ball should dribble and shield it, attempting to reach either of the corner cones (5-4). If successful, a point is awarded. Once the player with the ball has had one touch, the opponent can enter the grid to prevent a point being scored. The opponent gets a point for winning the ball.

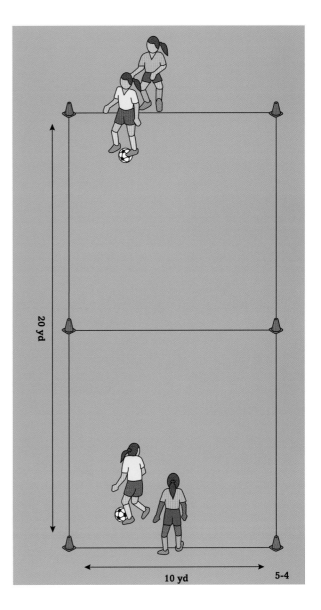

20 yd

10 yd

5-4

DRIBBLING–SHIELDIN

FIELD SIZE 20-yd x 20-yd grid.

ORGANIZATION 12 players, one soccer ball, four cones. Ten players are situated on the outside of the grid. The other two on the inside play one-on-one, using the players on the outside for passing situations, using one and two touches (5-5). The aim is to get possession of the ball by passing and shielding and trying to get behind the defender.

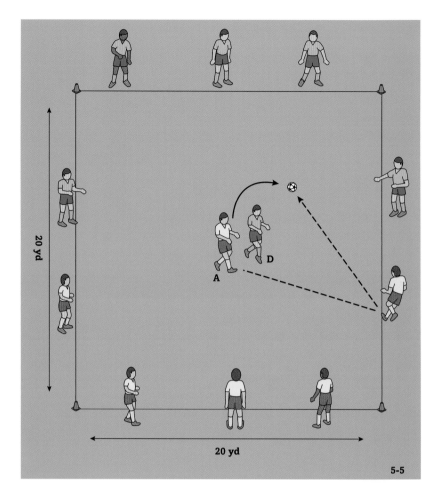

20 yd

20 yd

A

D

5-5

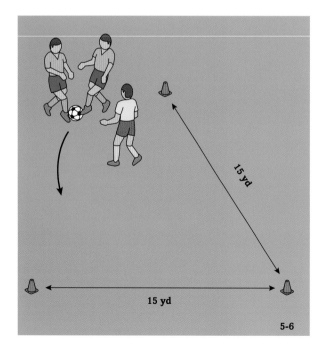

15 yd

15 yd

5-6

DRIBBLING–TURNING

FIELD SIZE 15-yd x 15-yd grid.

ORGANIZATION One-on-one-on-one, one soccer ball, three cones. Each player attempts to gain possession of the ball (5-6). When possession is gained, the player must try to score a goal by knocking down one of the cones.

FIELD SIZE 10-yd x 10-yd grids.

ORGANIZATION 14 players, eight soccer balls, 15 cones. Each one of the defending players is situated on the far line of a 10-yd grid and can only challenge for the ball when the attacking player enters their grid (5-7). The attacking players commence the practice by attempting to dribble the ball through each grid, past the defender, until they reach the other end or lose it to a defender (5-8). The ball is then dribbled back to the start on the outside of the grids.

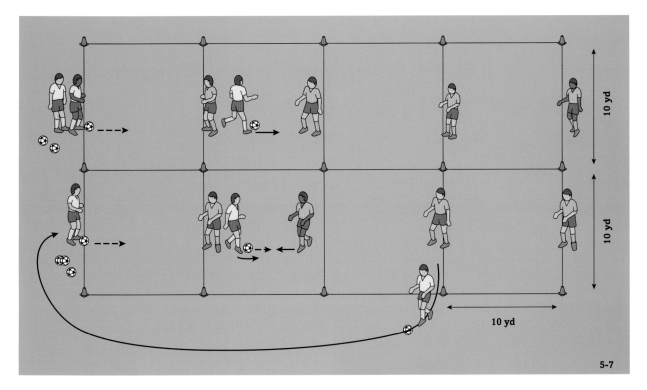

5-7

5-8

KICKING–INSIDE OF THE FOOT–PASSING

FIELD SIZE 20-yd x 10-yd grid.

ORGANIZATION Four groups of four, two soccer balls, four cones. Each player in turn plays the ball to the player diagonally opposite, then runs to the back of the adjacent line of players (5-9).

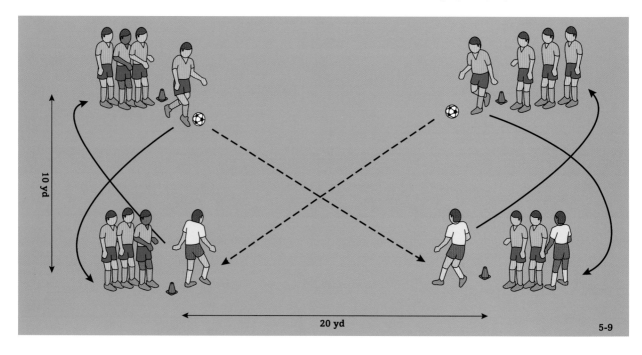

10 yd

20 yd

5-9

KICKING–INSIDE OF THE FOOT–PASSING

FIELD SIZE 30-yd x 30-yd grid.

ORGANIZATION Players numbered 1 to 7. Players move around inside grid while passing the ball in numerical order using the inside of the foot (5-10).

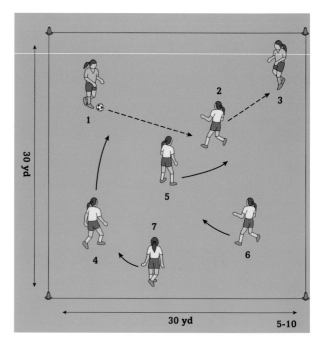

30 yd

30 yd

5-10

KICKING–INSIDE OF THE FOOT–PASSING

FIELD SIZE 10-yd x 10-yd grid.

ORGANIZATION Five players, one soccer ball, four cones. Play four-on-one; first pass is free. The four players towards the outside of the grid use one and two touches and try to keep the ball away from the defender in the middle of the grid (5-11). If a player near the outside misses the ball, that player becomes the defender, or the coach can set a time limit.

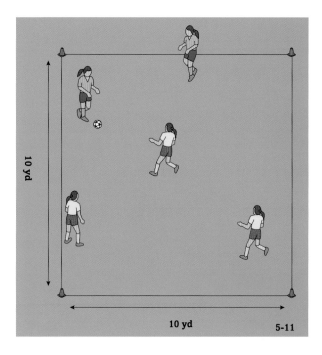

10 yd

10 yd

5-11

5-12

KICKING–INSIDE OF THE FOOT–PASSING

FIELD SIZE 30 yds long.

ORGANIZATION Four players per group, one soccer ball per group, two cones per group. To start the practice, using the inside of the foot, the end player plays the ball to the third player who passes it using one touch to the second player, who also uses one touch to pass it to the fourth player (5-12). This player has two touches: one to control the ball and the other to repeat the exercise. The coach can make this exercise into a competitive game by playing the groups against each other.

KICKING–INSIDE OF THE FOOT–PASSING

FIELD SIZE 10-yd x 10-yd grid.

ORGANIZATION Three-on-one. The three players towards the outside of the grid pass among themselves and move into open spaces to achieve maximum time and space. They try to keep the ball away from the defender in the middle of the grid (5-13). If a player near the outside misses the ball, that player becomes the defender, or the coach can set a time limit. This practice should help players understand short support.

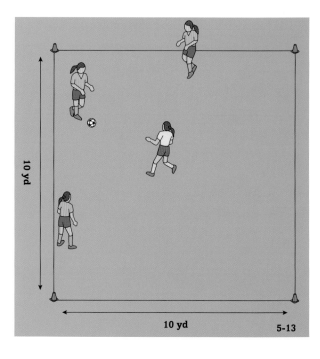

10 yd

10 yd

5-13

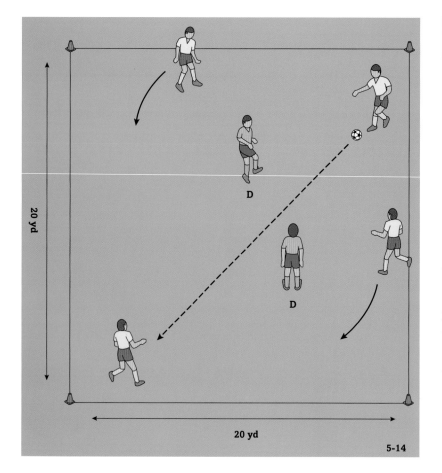

20 yd

20 yd

D

D

5-14

KICKING–INSIDE OF THE FOOT–PASSING

FIELD SIZE 20-yd x 20-yd grid.

ORGANIZATION Four-on-two. The four players on the outside of the grid pass the ball and move into open spaces to achieve maximum time and space. They try to keep the ball away from the two defenders in the middle of the grid (5-14). If a player on the outside misses the ball, that player becomes the defender-or the coach can set a time limit. This practice should help players understand short and long support and penetration (splitting the two defenders).

KICKING–VOLLEYS

FIELD SIZE Half a field.

ORGANIZATION Split the team into groups, A and B, with one target player on the edge of the penalty box and a goalkeeper in goal. A player from group A commences the practice by chipping a long pass to the target player, who lays the ball off to a play from group B, who is running forwards to shoot on goal (5-15). After each shot the players should rotate clockwise.

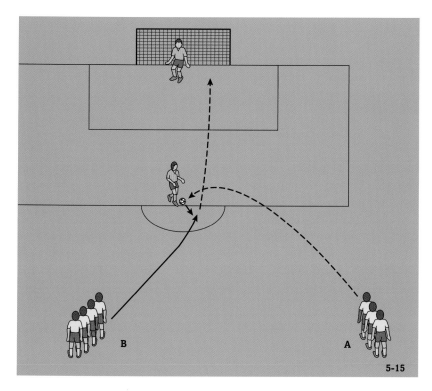

5-15

KICKING–VOLLEYS–SHOOTING

FIELD SIZE 10-yd x 10-yd grid in the attacking third of the field.

ORGANIZATION Players in pairs, one soccer ball per pair, four cones. One player from each pair stands behind the 10-yd x 10-yd grid facing the goal. The partner stands behind the goal line with a ball (5-16). The player with the ball punts it from the hands to a partner who controls the ball either out of the air or following one bounce inside the grid, using one of the six controlling surfaces. The player with the ball then takes a shot on goal. After each attempt, these players go to the back of the opposite group. The coach can make this exercise into a competitive game by playing two-on-two.

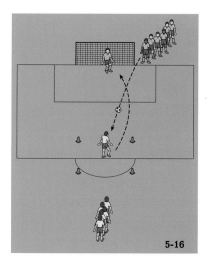

5-16

KICKING–LOFTED PASSING

FIELD SIZE Three 30-yd x 20-yd grids.

ORGANIZATION Nine players, one soccer ball, eight cones. Split the grid size into three equal areas with three players in each. The players at each end pass the ball to one another and to the players at the far end. The players in the middle area try to anticipate and intercept the passes (5-17). Limit the players at each end to two touches and only three passes. Points are scored for a good pass from one end to the other, and the players in the middle get a point if a pass is intercepted and controlled.

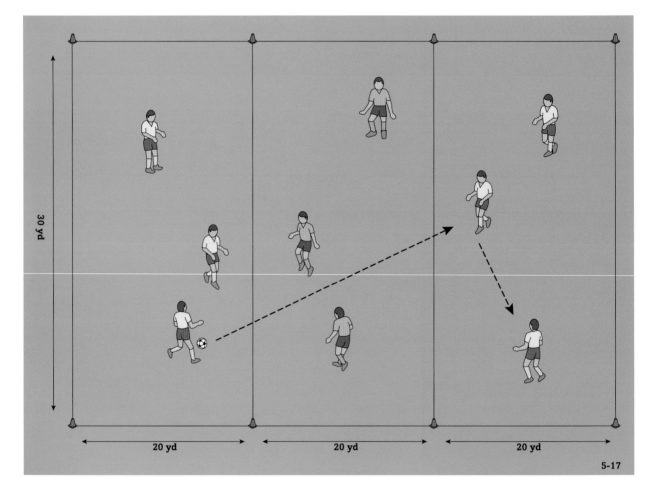

30 yd

20 yd 20 yd 20 yd

5-17

KICKING–LOFTED PASSING–CROSSING

FIELD SIZE Attacking-third of the field.

ORGANIZATION Players in five groups, a number of soccer balls, four cones. Two groups are positioned at each side of the field with the balls. These players dribble the ball down the touch line and make a cross into the near or far post area (5-18). The two groups on the outside of the center group—all positioned outside of the penalty box—make runs to the near and far post areas to shoot on goal. A player from the center group acts as a third attacker and moves forward into the middle of the penalty area, should the cross be too deep.

5-18

KICKING–LOFTED PASSING–CROSSING

FIELD SIZE Attacking-third of the field.

ORGANIZATION Players in six groups, a number of soccer balls, six cones. The ball is played from a wide midfield player to a player situated outside the field (5-19). This player plays the ball back to the midfielder who plays it into space (a double pass) for the wide player to run onto and cross either to the far or near post areas. The players from the groups situated in the center can either make a bent or cross-over run to the post areas and shoot on goal. The same exercise is conducted by the players on the other side of the field.

5-19

FIELD SIZE Full field.

ORGANIZATION Players in six groups, two goal-keepers, a number of soccer balls, two cones. The coach is positioned in the center circle with the soccer balls and plays a ball out to a wide player who dribbles it down the touch line and crosses it to the near post area (5-20). The group positioned on the edge of the penalty box runs to that area while the group positioned wide on that side runs to the far post area in an attempt on goal. The exercise is repeated at the opposite end of the field.

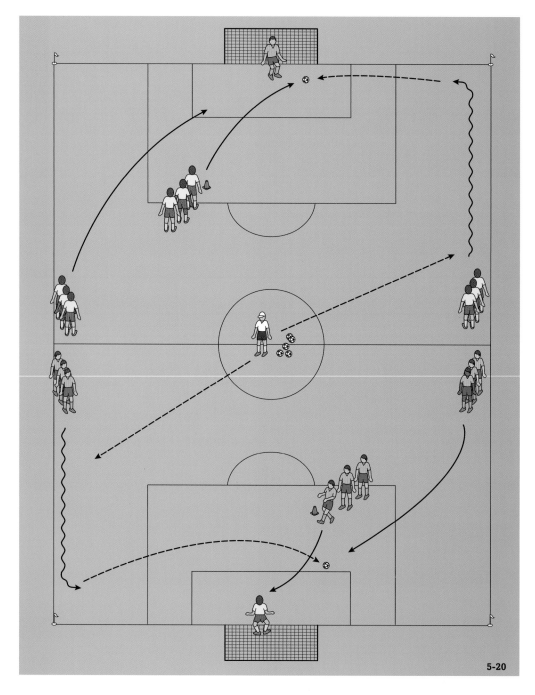

5-20

GROUND CONTROL

FIELD SIZE 30 yds long.

ORGANIZATION Players in groups of four, one soccer ball and two cones per group. Make sure that the players at each end stay behind the line. One of the end players commences the practice by passing the ball to the next player in line; this player must come to meet the ball, turn, and with one touch pass it to the next player in line (5-21). This is repeated until the ball reaches the player at the far end who has two touches: one to control and the other to pass back and repeat the exercise.

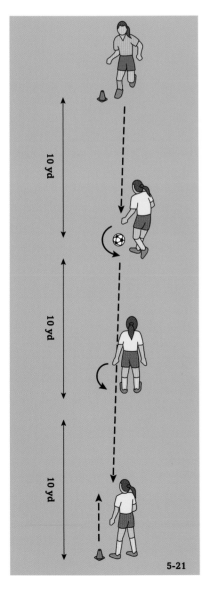

5-21

CONTROL—LOFTED PASSING

FIELD SIZE 30-yd x 10-yd grids.

ORGANIZATION Three players and one soccer ball per group, eight cones. The player at one end of the grid chips the ball to one of the other players at the other end of the grid (5-22). The receiver controls the ball inside the grid and then passes it to the partner, who chips it back to the server. The server in turn controls it and returns it to a player in the far grid. Continue the exercise.

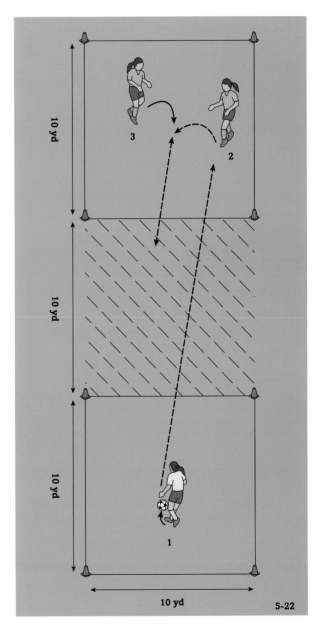

5-22

AERIAL CONTROL

FIELD SIZE 30 yds x 10 yds.

ORGANIZATION Players in pairs with one soccer ball per pair, eight cones. The ball is played to a partner to control and chip back (5-23). The exercise should be repeated by trapping the ball using all of the six body surfaces (5-24). The body must be in line with the ball and an early decision must be made as to the surface to use. The ball must be caught for a point after controlling it with one of the six body surfaces.

5-24 a

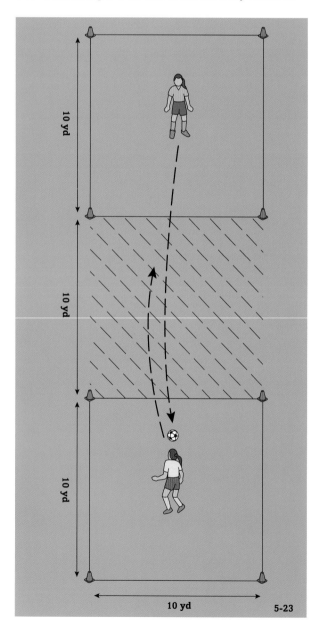

10 yd

10 yd

10 yd

10 yd

5-23

5-24 b

AERIAL CONTROL

FIELD SIZE 13 yds x 5 yds.

ORGANIZATION Players in pairs, one soccer ball per pair, eight cones. The first player punts the ball from inside the grid to a player in the opposite end of the grid, who controls it using one of the six controlling surfaces—either out of the air, or allowing only one bounce on the ground (5-25). The ball is then played back, and the exercise repeated.

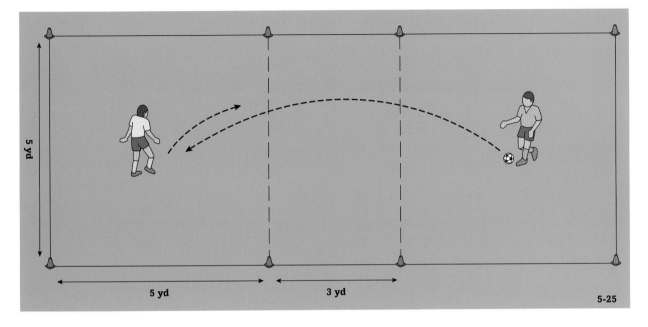

5 yd

5 yd   3 yd

5-25

AERIAL CONTROL

ORGANIZATION Players in pairs, one soccer ball per pair. The players stand opposite one another, 10 yards apart (5-26). The practice starts with one player taking a proper throw-in to the receiving partner, who must control the ball out of the air using one of the six controlling surfaces, and then play it back on the second touch.

PROGRESSION When the ball is returned to the thrower, it must be controlled out of the air and caught for a point.

step 1

step 2

step 3

5-26

AERIAL CONTROL

FIELD SIZE 40 yds x 20 yds.

ORGANIZATION 10 players, two teams of five, one soccer ball per team, 15 cones. Team members place themselves one in each grid and two outside at one end (5-27). The outside player punts the ball to the player in the first grid who must control, turn, and gently volley the ball to the player in the next part of the grid. This is repeated until the ball reaches the player in the last section of the grid, who controls and catches it for a point. If the ball hits the ground or a team member leaves a grid, the team must start over.

PROGRESSION Two touch, three touch, using only the designated body surfaces.

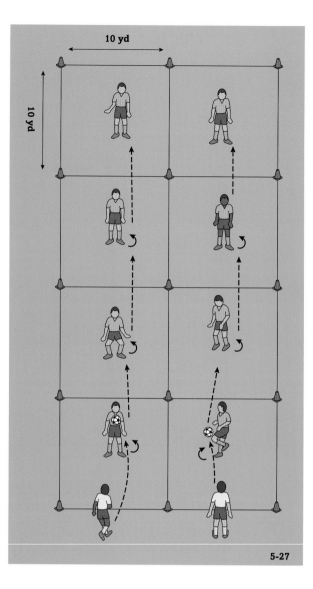

5-27

AERIAL CONTROL

FIELD SIZE Attacking-third of field.

ORGANIZATION Players in pairs, one soccer ball per pair. The first two players of each group commence the practice when one player bounces the ball, then kicks it in the air to a partner (5-28). The partner allows it to bounce, then controls it using one of the six controlling surfaces. Following another bounce it is played to the partner, who has run past. The exercise is repeated until either partner can take a shot on goal. We recommend that a goalkeeper not be used. The ball must hit the goal net on the full (fly) to score. If either of the partners makes a mistake on the way to goal, that player returns to the back of the group and the exercise is repeated by the next two players in line.

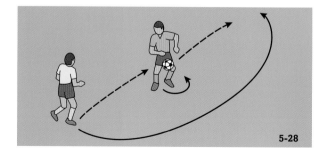

5-28

AERIAL CONTROL

ORGANIZATION Players in groups of four, one soccer ball per group. The first player bounces the ball, then passes it in the air to the next player who must control, using the chest and thigh, before turning and passing it on (5-29). This pattern is repeated backwards and forwards along the line of players.

5-29

HEADING—ATTACKING

FIELD SIZE The center circle.

ORGANIZATION Players in pairs, one soccer ball per pair, 10 cones. Players form a circle, facing a partner. Ten cones are placed in the middle of the circle. One player chips the ball over the cones to a partner, who must head the ball in an attempt to knock over the cones (5-30). Players change roles every 10 tries.

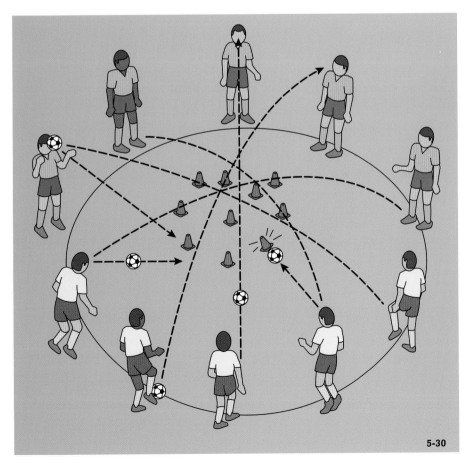

5-30

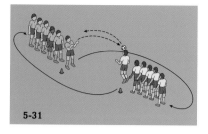

5-31

HEADING—DEFENDING

ORGANIZATION Players in two groups, one soccer ball, two cones. Two cones are placed ten yards apart with a group of players at each cone. The practice starts with the first player serving the ball underhand to the front player of the group opposite, then running to the back of that group (5-31). The receiving player heads the ball back to the next player of the opposite group, then runs to the back of that group. The exercise is repeated with the remaining players heading the ball back and forth and running to the end of the opposite group. If the ball hits the ground, the exercise is restarted from the beginning.

HEADING—PASSING

ORGANIZATION Four players, two soccer balls. One of the players with a ball throws it underhand to the receiving player, who heads to the player without a ball (5-32). The other player with the ball repeats the exercise, and play continues (5-33).

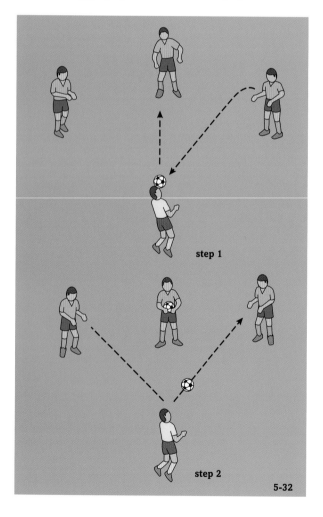

step 1

step 2

5-32

5-33

GOALKEEPING *(Basic Handling)*

FIELD SIZE 10-yd x 10-yd grid.

ORGANIZATION Two players and a goalkeeper, two soccer balls, four cones. Position the goalkeeper in the middle of the grid facing the first server. The ball is thrown underhand at varying heights to the goalkeeper, who gathers and returns it to the first server before spinning around to receive the next ball thrown by the second server (5-34).

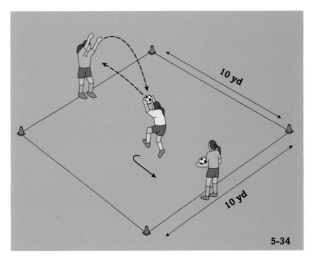

5-34

GOALKEEPING *(Basic Handling)*

ORGANIZATION Goalkeeper, one player, a number of soccer balls. The goalkeeper stands in the middle of the goal on the goal line, facing away from the server, who stands six yards from the goalkeeper (5-35). The server calls the side that the ball is to be served to and the goalkeeper must react by turning and saving it.

5-35

GOALKEEPING *(Basic Handling)*

ORGANIZATION Goalkeeper, two players, a number of soccer balls. The goalkeeper stands in the middle of the goal on the goal line. One player stands on the goal line with the balls, near the edge of the six-yard box, and throws a ball underhand in the air to the other player standing six yards out from the center of the goal (5-36). The ball is gently volleyed using the inside of the foot to the goalkeeper, who makes a save and returns it to the server. The exercise is repeated. Ensure that the shots played to the goalkeeper are not struck too hard. As in all practices, adjust to the goalkeeper's abilities.

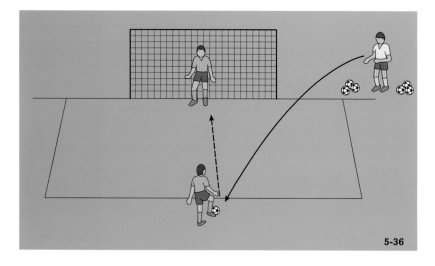

5-36

GOALKEEPING
(Shot Stopping)

ORGANIZATION Goalkeeper, one player, a number of soccer balls. The goalkeeper stands in the center of the goal on the goal line. The other player stands six to eight yards out in front of the goal with a supply of balls (5-37). Using the inside of the foot, the player serves a ball along the ground one yard to the side of the goalkeeper, who drops to save it. The exercise is repeated to the goalkeeper's opposite side.

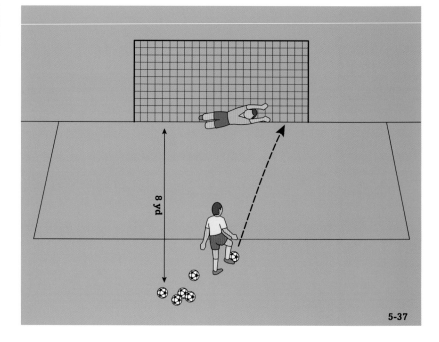

8 yd

5-37

GOALKEEPING *(Shot Stopping)*

ORGANIZATION Goalkeeper, two players, one soccer ball. The goalkeeper positions himself on his knees six yards from the server, who throws the ball above the goalkeeper's head (5-38). The goalkeeper, using both hands, should palm it over an imaginary crossbar. The second player catches it and returns it to the server.

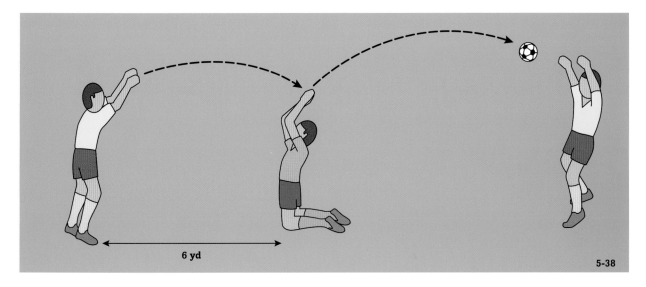

6 yd

5-38

GOALKEEPING *(Shot Stopping)*

ORGANIZATION Goalkeeper, one player, a number of soccer balls. The goalkeeper stands in the middle of the goal on the goal line. As the goalkeeper advances forward towards the six-yard line, the server volleys a ball just above the goalkeeper's head (5-39). The goalkeeper should flex the knees, angle back, and deflect the ball over the crossbar using both hands.

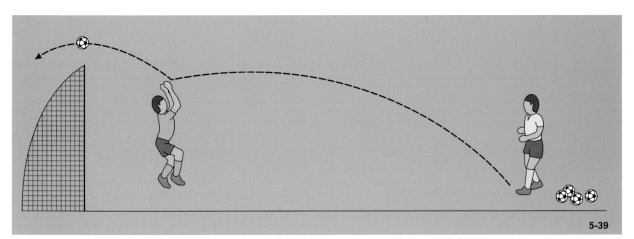

5-39

ORGANIZATION Two players, goalkeeper with a number of soccer balls, four cones. The goalkeeper takes a dead-ball kick (goal kick) and attempts to play the ball through two cones spaced 10 yards apart and 25 yards from the goal line. The ball must pass through the cones on the full (5-40). Have players attempt 10 goal kicks from each side of the goal. As efficiency improves, increase the distance accordingly.

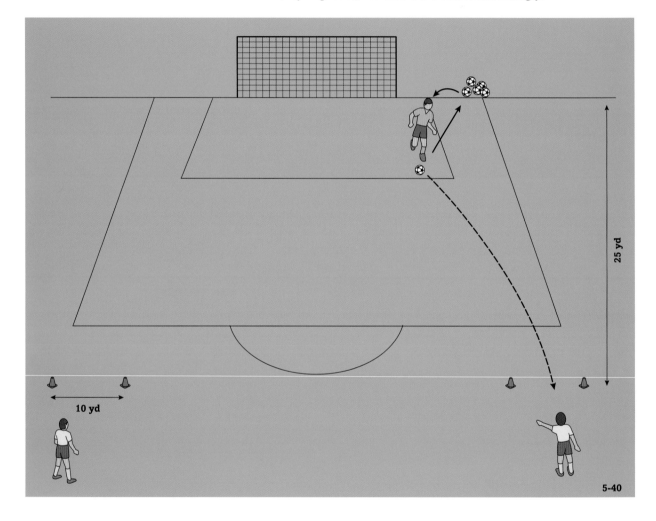

10 yd

25 yd

5-40

ORGANIZATION Goalkeeper, one player with a number of soccer balls, six cones. The serving player plays the ball to the goalkeeper, who collects it on the edge of the penalty area and distributes it using either a punt or an overarm throw through any of three sets of cones (5-41). Each set of cones is positioned across the pitch, 15 yards apart and 40 yards out from the goal line. The ball may bounce prior to going through the cones.

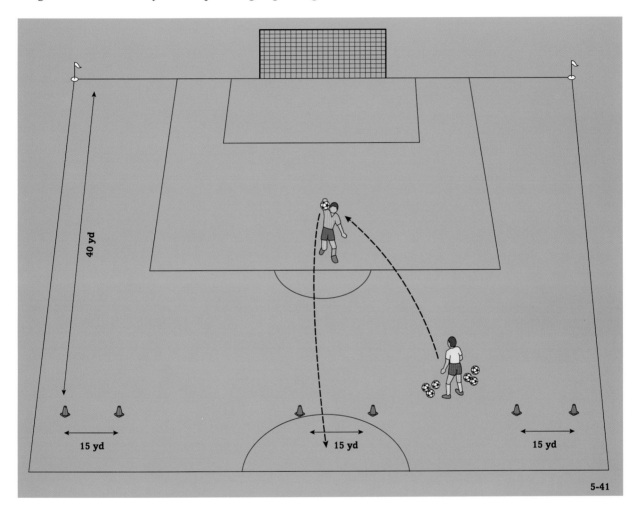

5-41

ORGANIZATION Goalkeeper, one player with a number of soccer balls, 14 cones. The goalkeeper receives a ball played in by the serving player and distributes it through any of the sets of cones (5-42). The goalkeeper should use a punt (volley), a dropkick (half-volley), or a throw (overarm, javelin, underarm). Vary the serve so that the goalkeeper can use all of the techniques required for good distribution. The ball may contact the ground prior to passing through the cones.

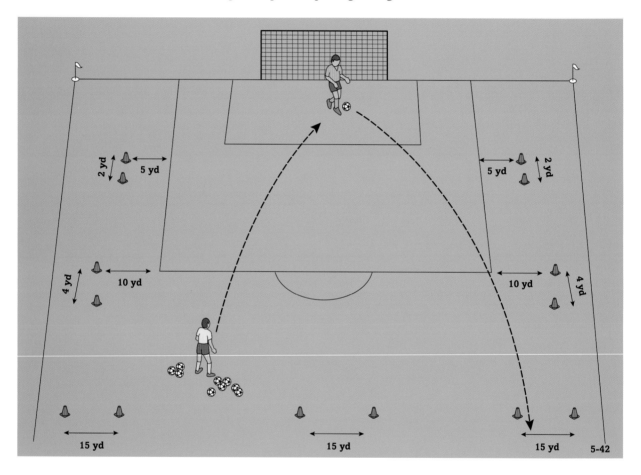

5-42

ORGANIZATION Goalkeeper, one player with a number of soccer balls. The serving player stands at one side on the edge of the six-yard area. The server throws a ball gently to the goalkeeper, who collects it in the air, pulls it down into the chest, and then returns it to the server (5-43). Encourage the goalkeeper to attack the ball down a route which allows for the earliest possible contact. After 10 serves, players change sides.

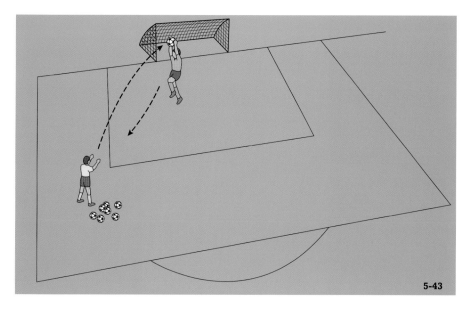

5-43

ORGANIZATION Goalkeeper, two or three players with a number of soccer balls. The two serving players are positioned one on each side of the penalty area and 12 yards out from the goal line. Position the goalkeeper in the six-yard box. Each server in turn throws the ball overarm for the goalkeeper to collect (5-44). If the goalkeeper shows confidence when collecting the crosses, add a passive opponent in the six-yard box. Encourage the goalkeeper to call "keepers" when collecting the crosses.

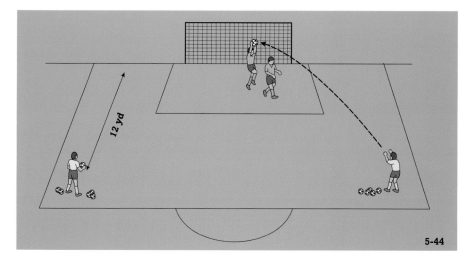

5-44

ORGANIZATION Goalkeeper; four players, two with a number of soccer balls. Position the goalkeeper in the goal with two other players, one as an opponent and the other as a teammate. The other two players should be positioned as servers just inside the penalty box (5-45). As each ball is served in from alternate sides, the goalkeeper must call and decide whether to catch or punch it, depending on the positions of the other players. Encourage the goalkeeper to communicate early to prevent defensive mistakes from developing.

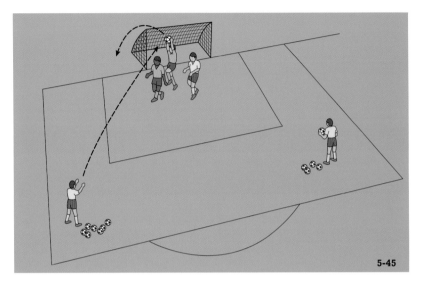

5-45

ORGANIZATION Goalkeeper; three players, each with a soccer ball. Position the three players around the penalty area (5-46). On the command from the coach, the goalkeeper advances toward the nominated player and attempts to narrow the angle and to make the save before recovering to repeat the exercise.

5-46

ORGANIZATION One player and a goalkeeper with a number of soccer balls. The goalkeeper (who is positioned in the goal) serves the ball out to the player on the edge of the penalty box, who is limited to two touches (5-47). As the player plays the ball at varying angles with the first touch, the goalkeeper readjusts position and narrows the angle to receive the shot.

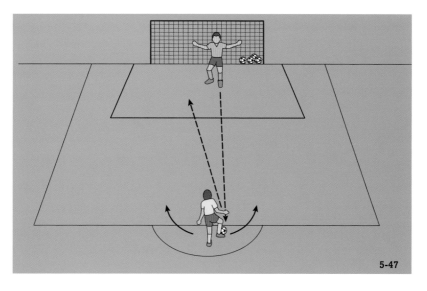

5-47

ORGANIZATION Goalkeeper, three players, one with a number of soccer balls. Position the goalkeeper in the middle of the six-yard box. The server, stationed to one side of the goal, plays the ball out to either of the players on the edge of the penalty area inside the "D." The players can pass back and forth, dribble on the goalkeeper, or shoot (5-48). The goalkeeper must decide whether to advance and/or readjust sideways to narrow the angle and make the save. The goalkeeper must reposition after the shot is made to repeat the exercise.

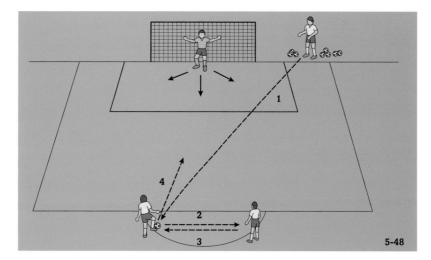

5-48

Team Games

FIELD SIZE 30 yds x 20 yds.

ORGANIZATION Three-on-two and two-on-three grid game. To score, the attacking player must dribble or pass the ball through the small goals (5-49). If a defending player wins the ball, it must be passed quickly to an attacking partner in the other half of the grid. When a goal is scored, the ball goes to a defender for a free pass. Players change roles every five goals.

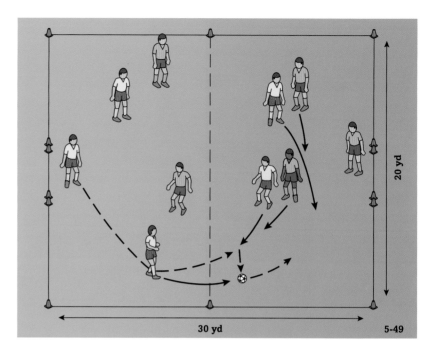

20 yd

30 yd

5-49

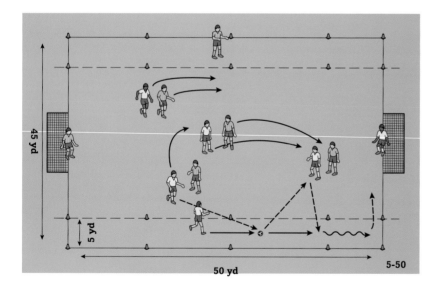

45 yd

5 yd

50 yd

5-50

FIELD SIZE 50 yds x 45 yds.

ORGANIZATION Four-on-four plus goalkeepers and two wide neutral players. The wide players must stay in their zone, but can be used by the team in possession of the ball to advance down the field (5-50).

PROGRESSION Play three-on-three plus goalkeepers, but add another two wide players with the restriction that they can receive the ball only in their half of the field (5-51). After a challenge, they must get back quickly.

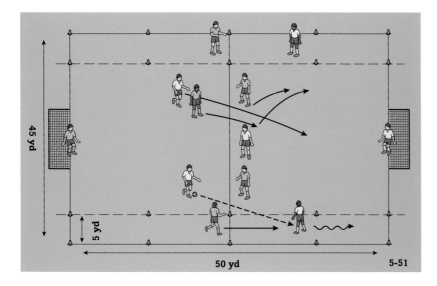

45 yd

5 yd

50 yd

5-51

TEAM GAMES—KEEP AWAY

TEAM GAMES—KEEP AWAY

FIELD SIZE 60 yds x 40 yds.

ORGANIZATION Team players, one soccer ball, four cones. Play the keep-away games (5-52) in combination of six-on-four, five-on-five, six-on-six, or seven-on-seven.

TEAM GAMES—KEEP AWAY

FIELD SIZE Half of the field.

ORGANIZATION Six-on-six. To score a point, the team in possession must dribble the ball over the half-way line or goal line (5-53).

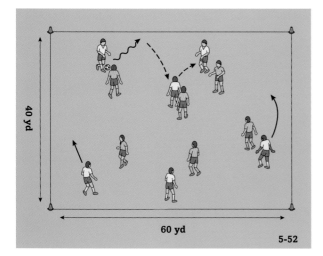

40 yd

60 yd

5-52

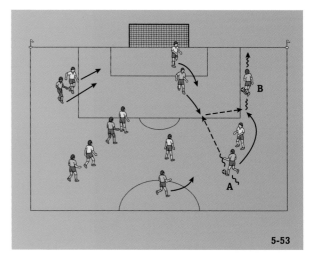

5-53

Chapter 6

U-15 Drills & Practices

(under age 15)

*A*t this age level, your emphasis shifts from small-sided games to a concentration on small group practices—five-on-five through to seven-on-seven. The focus of these group practices converges on team formations and shape.

Practices

ORGANIZATION Players in pairs, one soccer ball per pair. One player sits down while the other juggles the ball. The coach designates one of the six controlling surfaces. The juggling player kicks the ball up in the air for the sitting player to rise and control with the nominated surface (6-1). Repeat exercise alternating roles.

Length of Training Session:
90 MINUTES

Warm-up 10 minutes
Technique/Skill Development 20 minutes
Team Games/Set Plays 40 minutes
Free Play 20 minutes

step 1   step 2   step 3

6-1

WARM-UP

FIELD SIZE 15-yd. x 15-yd grids.

ORGANIZATION Two groups with players numbered one to seven in each, one soccer ball per group, eight cones. Commence the practice with both teams in their own grid passing the ball freely. The coach nominates two players by number to enter the opponent's grid and attempt to win the ball during a period of two minutes (6-2). Then another two players are nominated and the first two return to their grid. The exercise is repeated and the score is kept by counting the number of successful passes and intercepts.

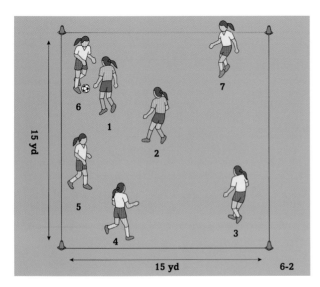

15 yd

15 yd   6-2

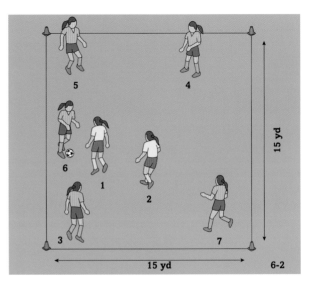

15 yd

15 yd   6-2

DRIBBLING

FIELD SIZE Attacking-third of field.

ORGANIZATION Players in groups of six, one server with a number of soccer balls, one goalkeeper, two cones. The server plays the ball over the goal. One player from each group runs forward to challenge for it (6-3). The player that wins the ball first becomes the attacker, and the other the defender. The attacker attempts to beat the defender and score a goal. The coach should encourage players to control the ball quickly, shield properly, and shoot when an opportunity arises.

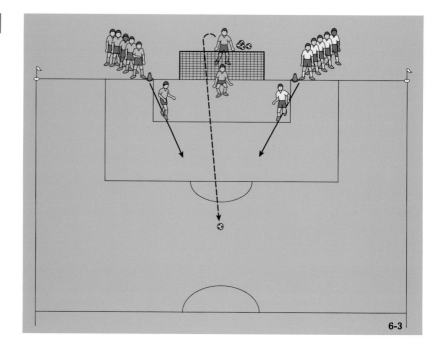

6-3

DRIBBLING

FIELD SIZE Half of the field.

ORGANIZATION Four groups of players plus a goalkeeper, a number of soccer balls, four cones. The two groups on the goal line have the soccer balls. A ball is driven along the ground towards a player on the halfway line (6-4). The receiving player runs forward, controls, and dribbles the ball towards goal, attempting to beat the server by dribbling around them, finishing with a shot on goal. Following each attempt, the players go to the back of the opposite group.

PROGRESSION Play the ball in the air to the receiver.

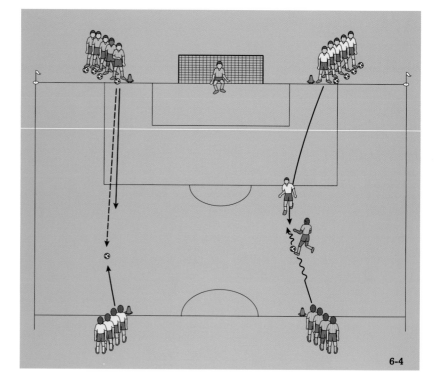

6-4

DRIBBLING

FIELD SIZE Half of the field.
ORGANIZATION Two groups of players plus two goalkeepers, a number of soccer balls. Two portable goals are placed on the edge of the penalty box. The defending players stand between the goals. The group of attacking players is positioned in the center circle with the soccer balls. The attacker dribbles the ball forward and attempts to beat the defender and take a shot on either goal (6-5).

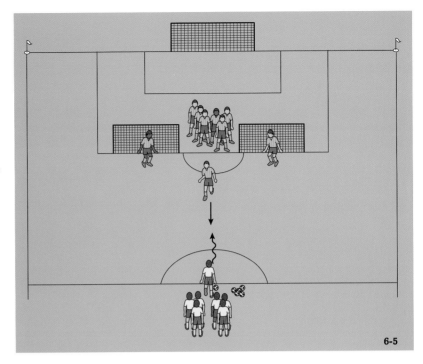

6-5

DRIBBLING

FIELD SIZE 50 yds x 44 yds.
ORGANIZATION One-on-one plus a goalkeeper in each half of the area, one soccer ball, six cones. The player with the ball passes it to an attacking team player in the other half of the area. The attacker controls and attempts to dribble around the opponent and score (6-6). If the opponent wins the ball, it should be played back to the other end for a quick counterattack.

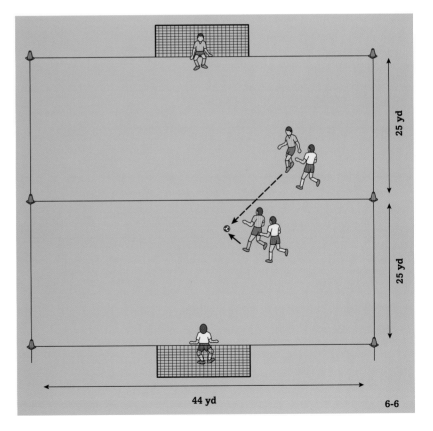

25 yd

25 yd

44 yd

6-6

KICKING—SHOOTING

FIELD SIZE Penalty box.

ORGANIZATION Set up cones 16 yards from the goal and six yards apart. The shooting player dribbles to the cone, performs a feint (deceptive move), beats the cone to the outside, and finishes with a shot on a goal (6-7).

VARIATIONS

- Attack the cone to the inside.
- Attack the cone from either side.
- Dribble diagonally to the far cone.

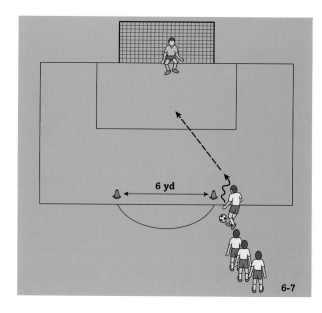

6-7

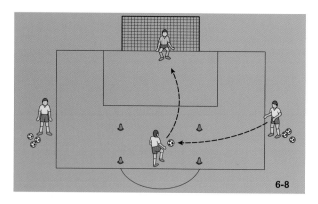

6-8

KICKING—SHOOTING

FIELD SIZE Penalty box.

ORGANIZATION Groups of three plus a goalkeeper, a number of soccer balls, four cones placed 10 yards by 10 yards apart in the center of the penalty box. The serving players alternately serve balls on the ground or in the air to the shooting player (6-8). Restrict the shooter to two touches. Emphasize concentration and hitting the target.

KICKING—SHOOTING

FIELD SIZE Penalty box.

ORGANIZATION Two groups of eight plus a goalkeeper, a number of soccer balls. The coach serves a ball from the edge of the "D" into the penalty box (6-9). The player that wins the ball can either shoot or pass to another teammate for a shot on goal.

PROGRESSION The players must make three passes before taking a shot. Players must make a wall pass before taking a shot.

6-9

KICKING—SHOOTING

FIELD SIZE Penalty box.

ORGANIZATION Players in pairs, a number of soccer balls. The two players in the penalty box play together as a partnership; one player will be the target and the other will shoot (6-10). After one minute they change roles. The players on the outside alternate by playing ground or air balls into the target player, who lays them off for the shooter to shoot on the first touch. After two minutes, change partnerships.

6-10

KICKING—VOLLEYS

FIELD SIZE Attacking-third of field.

ORGANIZATION Five players plus a goalkeeper, a number of soccer balls, four cones set out in a 10-yard x 10-yard grid in the penalty box. Four servers are numbered one to four, each with a supply of soccer balls. The coach calls a number, and the player in the grid looks towards that server to receive the pass, controls, then volleys the ball towards goal (6-11). Restrict the shooter to two touches. Emphasize concentration and hitting the target.

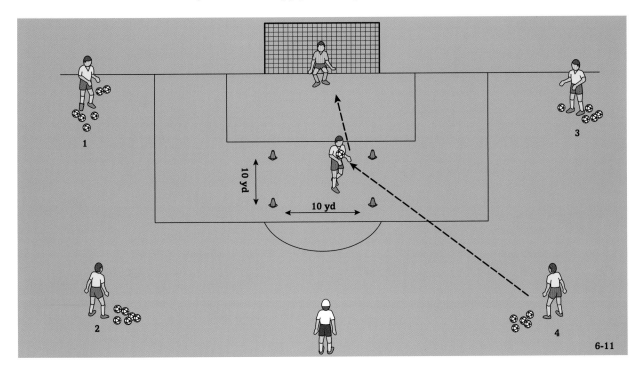

6-11

KICKING—VOLLEYS

FIELD SIZE 44 yds x 36 yds.

ORGANIZATION Five players plus two goalkeepers, a number of soccer balls, four cones set out in a 10-yard x 10-yard grid in the center of the playing area. Four servers are numbered one to four, each with a supply of soccer balls. The coach calls a number and the player in the grid looks towards that server to receive the pass, controls, then volleys the ball towards either goal (6-12). Emphasize concentration and hitting the target.

PROGRESSION

- The shooter must shoot towards the goal from the same end that the service came from.
- The shooter must shoot towards the goal on the opposite end from where the service came.
- The shooter must shoot on the second touch with a bounce.
- The shooter must shoot on the second touch without a bounce.
- The shooter must shoot on the first touch.

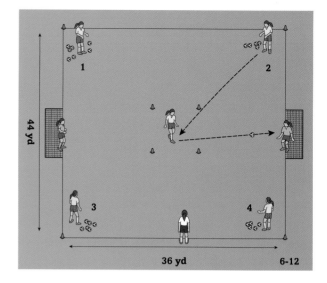

PASSING—CONTROL

FIELD SIZE 50-yd x 10-yd grid.

ORGANIZATION Groups of five, one soccer ball per group, eight cones. The end player chips the ball to player 3; this player plays the ball back along the ground to player 2 (6-13). Player 2 passes it along the ground to player 4 who plays it back to player 3. Player 3 then plays it to player 5, who lofts the ball back to the first player. All ground passes should be one touch, except for the end players, who have two touches.

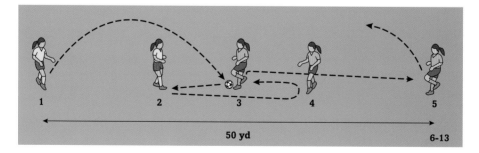

FIELD SIZE Half of the field.

ORGANIZATION 11 players plus a goalkeeper. The ball is served to a defender, who plays it back. The server then plays the ball into the space behind the defender for a wide player to run onto. The defender turns and tracks down the wide player and applies pressure to the cross. The other wide player runs to the near post (6-14) while the server makes a run to the far post. The coach can also vary the practice by having the server make a run to the near post while the other wide player makes a run to the far post.

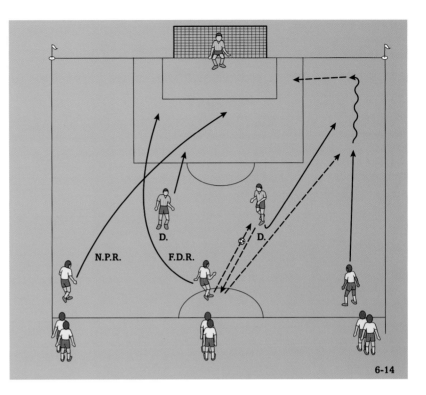

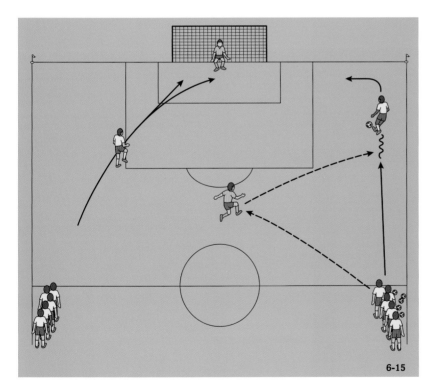

PASSING—CROSSES

FIELD SIZE Half of the field.

ORGANIZATION Two groups of players plus two goalkeepers, a number of soccer balls. A serving player chips the ball to the near goalkeeper, then makes a run down the line; the goalkeeper collects the ball, then redistributes it back to the server. The server controls and crosses either to the near or far post to a player from the opposite group who has run forward to shoot on goal (6-15). The exercise is repeated, and the goalkeepers are changed after each goal.

PROGRESSION Change teams over.

FIELD SIZE Full field.

ORGANIZATION Two groups of players plus two goalkeepers, a number of soccer balls. The coach is positioned in the center circle with the soccer balls, and two strikers are positioned in each penalty box. The coach serves a ball out to a wide player who controls it and moves forward down the touch line (6-16). Once close to the goal line, the player with the ball makes a 360-degree turn to represent a challenge or problem. Now the runners to the near or far post will have to make changes to their runs. The near post runner should turn away and reopen the near post space to allow the far post runner to run into, then loop towards, the far post. The new near post runner must attack the space at speed as the ball is crossed into the penalty area.

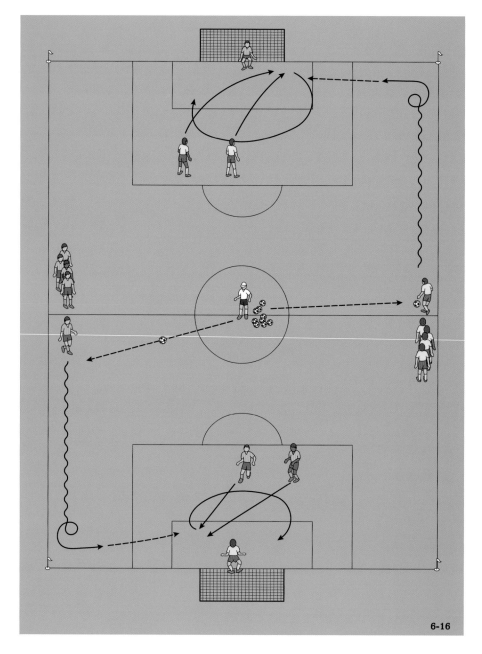

6-16

PASSING—CONTROL

FIELD SIZE 20-yd x 20-yd grid.

ORGANIZATION Eight players, one soccer ball, four cones. Five players with the ball attempt to keep it away from the other three (6-17). Any attacking player who makes a mistake or gives the ball away changes places with the defender who has been in the longest. Or the coach can instruct them to play a time-limited game of two minutes.

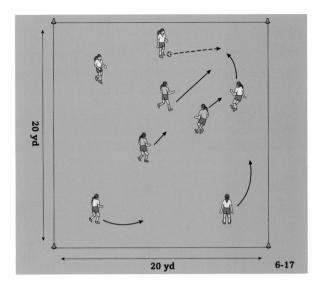

PASSING—LOFTED

FIELD SIZE 30-yd x 10-yd grid.

ORGANIZATION Players in pairs, one soccer ball per pair, eight cones. Playing two-on-two, commence the practice with a player passing the ball in the air across the middle grid to a player in the far grid. who must control and lay it off for a partner to play it back across (6-18). Repeat the exercise.

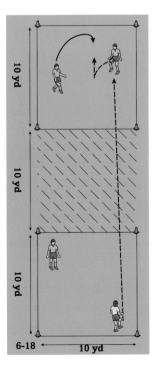

PASSING—CONTROL

FIELD SIZE 30-yd x 10-yd grid.

ORGANIZATION Eight players, one soccer ball, eight cones. Play the ball across the dead space into the opposite grid. Once it is under control, the three attackers must keep the ball away from the lone defender and set up a pass back across to the opposite grid (6-19). If the defender wins the ball, the player that made the mistake changes places.

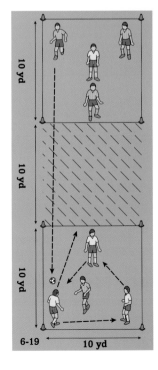

PASSING

FIELD SIZE 35-yd x 10-yd grid.

ORGANIZATION Four groups, two soccer balls, eight cones. The player with the ball passes it using the inside of the foot to the front player of the group opposite, then moves to the back of the team (6-20). The receiving player repeats the exercise.

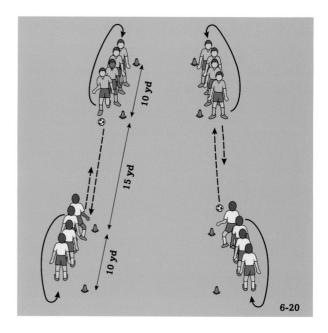

PASSING

FIELD SIZE 35-yd x 10-yd grid.

ORGANIZATION Four groups, two soccer balls, eight cones. The player with the ball passes it using the inside of the foot to the front player of the group opposite, then moves around the end cone to the back of that group (6-21). The receiving player repeats the exercise.

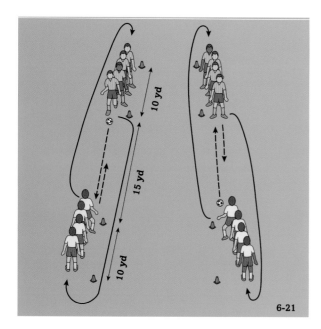

PASSING

FIELD SIZE 5-yd x 10-yd grid.

ORGANIZATION Four groups, two soccer balls, eight cones. The player with the ball passes it diagonally using the inside of the foot to the front player of the group diagonally opposite, then moves to the back of his own group (6-22). The receiving player repeats the exercise.

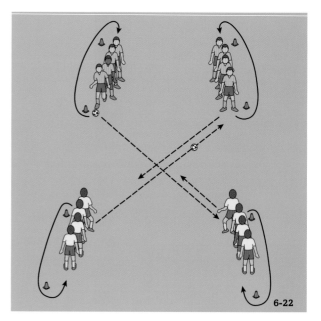

PASSING—CONTROL

FIELD SIZE 30-yd x 30-yd grid.

ORGANIZATION Eight players inside the grid, each with a soccer ball; eight players outside the grid; four cones. The players inside the grid dribble and pass the ball, performing wall passes and overlaps with the outside players (6-23). After a time frame, reverse the roles.

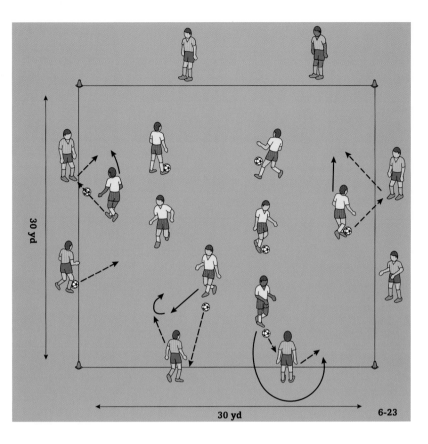

PASSING—CONTROL

FIELD SIZE 20-yd x 20-yd grid.

ORGANIZATION Four groups, two soccer balls, four cones. The player from the first group with the ball passes it forward and follows the pass, moving to the back of the receiving group. The receiving player controls the ball, turns, then passes it (6-24). The exercise is repeated. Encourage players to use either foot by reversing the direction of the practice.

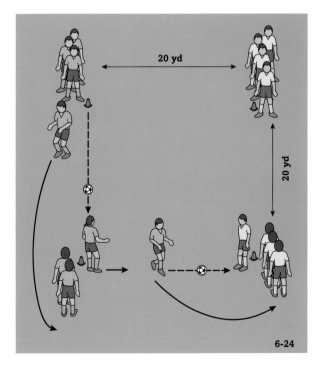

FIELD SIZE 80-yd x 40-yd grid.

ORGANIZATION Two groups of players numbered one to seven, two soccer balls, six cones. Each team must pass and control the ball in numerical order within their 40-yard by 40-yard grid (6-25).

PROGRESSION Remove the midline and allow both groups to play in the 80-yard by 40-yard area (6-26). This will provide unopposed obstruction, and players will have to deal with the opening and closing of space.

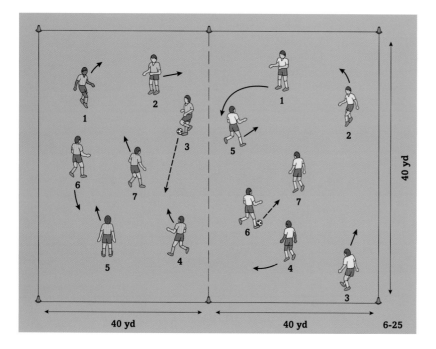

40 yd · 40 yd · 40 yd · 6-25

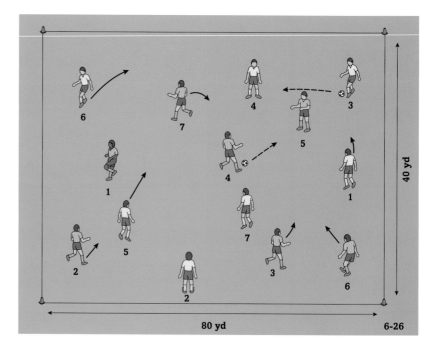

40 yd · 80 yd · 6-26

PASSING—CONTROL

FIELD SIZE 35-yd x 10-yd grid.

ORGANIZATION Four groups, two soccer balls, eight cones. The player plays the ball diagonally using the inside of the foot, then runs around to the back of the team diagonally opposite (6-27).

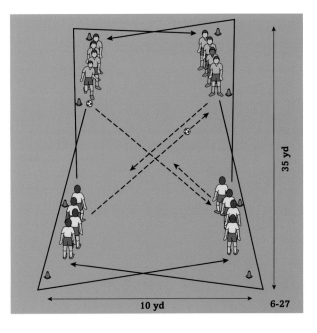

PASSING—CONTROL

FIELD SIZE 70-yd x 40-yd grid.

ORGANIZATION 10 players, one soccer ball, eight cones. Play three-on-three in the middle third. Each team has two target players in their attacking third. The players in the middle should attempt to create space, allowing a pass in the air to one of their target players (6-28). The player must control the ball and catch it for a point. The target players are free to move anywhere inside their third of the field.

PROGRESSION

- The attacker, with one touch, passes the ball to a partner to control and catch.
- The attacker, with one touch, passes the ball to a partner who shoots at goal with the first touch.
- The attacker controls, turns, and shoots at goal, with a two-touch total.

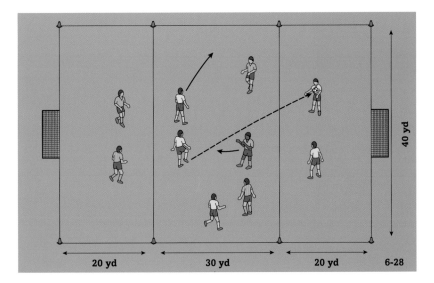

PASSING—INSIDE OF THE FOOT

FIELD SIZE 40-yd x 40-yd grid.

ORGANIZATION 14 players, one soccer ball, four cones. Four players from each team are positioned on the outside of the grid, three players from each team on the inside. Play three-on-three inside the grid; the players in possession of the ball can also use the outside team players if necessary to maintain possession (6-29). The players outside the grid can only use one touch to pass the ball back.

PROGRESSION When an outside player is in possession of the ball, the opposition player may apply pressure.

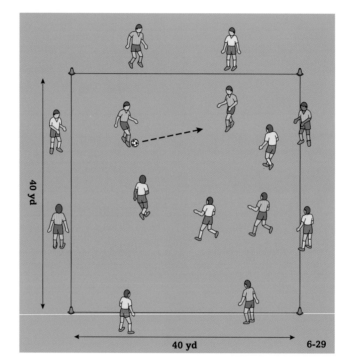

40 yd

40 yd

6-29

AERIAL CONTROL

FIELD SIZE 40-yd x 10-yd grid.

ORGANIZATION Players in groups of four, one soccer ball per group. The groups of players are positioned in a straight line. The first player throws the ball to the second player, who controls it on the chest and lays it back at an angle to the first player, who then chips the ball to the distant fourth player to catch (6-30). Step 2 is to repeat the exercise in reverse. The coach can make it a competitive game by playing the groups against each other.

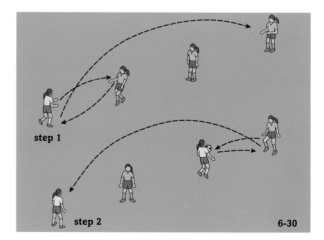

step 1

step 2

6-30

AERIAL CONTROL

FIELD SIZE 44 yds x 36 yds.

ORGANIZATION Players in numbered pairs, one soccer ball per pair; two goalkeepers. One player dribbles the ball while the partner moves around (6-31). When the coach designates a controlling surface, the ball is stopped and played in the air to the partner who controls it with that surface, as shown in 1, 3, 5, and 6. The controlling player dribbles the ball away.

PROGRESSION

- As a variation on the basic exercise, when the coach calls a number and the controlling surface to be used, the players advance to the goal area. The ball is played as in the first exercise, ending with a shot on goal as shown in 2 and 4.

- Double the number of partners, then have them go to either goal using 1-2s (wall passes) and combination plays, finishing with a shot.

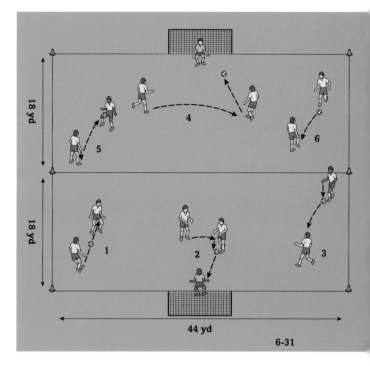

6-31

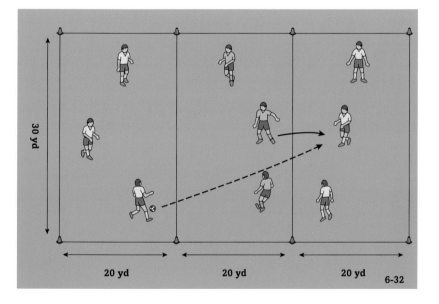

6-32

AERIAL CONTROL

FIELD SIZE 60-yd x 30-yd grid.

ORGANIZATION Nine players, one soccer ball, eight cones, three players per grid. The ball should be played in the air across the middle of the grid to the opposite end of the grid. Once it's controlled, the players must keep possession from a defender who has entered the grid (6-32). The ball should then be returned in the same manner to the opposite end, and the defender should return to the middle. Another defender applies pressure at the opposite end.

HEADING

FIELD SIZE Penalty box.

ORGANIZATION Six players, one goalkeeper, a number of soccer balls. Four players, each with several soccer balls, take turns serving them one at a time to the two attacking players to head in an attempt to score (6-33).

PROGRESSION

- Add one more defender.
- Add two more defenders.
- Add a third attacker.
- Add a third defender.

Coaching Points

- Head the ball into the goal in the direction that it came from.
- Head the ball down and away from the goalkeeper.
- Head the ball back across the face of the goal if a direct header cannot be taken.

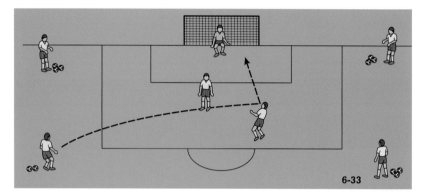

6-33

HEADING

FIELD SIZE 60 yds x 40 yds.

ORGANIZATION 10 players, two goalkeepers, one soccer ball, four cones. Practice commences with a player throwing the ball in the air to a teammate, who heads to another member of the team, who catches it (6-34). The sequence is: throw, head, catch. Any interception by the opposing players must be done in this sequence. A goal can be scored only when the ball is headed.

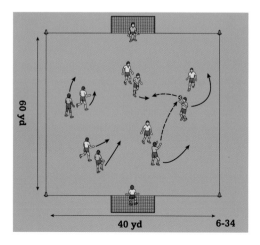

60 yd

40 yd

6-34

HEADING

FIELD SIZE Full width x 40 yds.

ORGANIZATION 10 players, two goalkeepers, a number of soccer balls, 16 cones. The server passes the ball to a wide player who moves down the wing (6-35). The wide player crosses the ball to either the near or far post as the attacking players time their runs in an attempt to head and score.

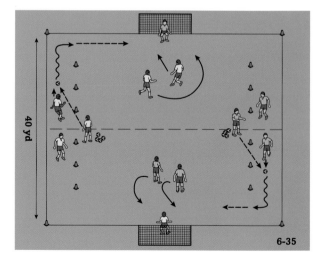

40 yd

6-35

GOALKEEPING *(Handling—Ground and Air Shots)*

ORGANIZATION Goalkeeper, one player with a number of soccer balls. The goalkeeper stands in the middle of the goal. The server stands at the edge of the penalty area and drives ground and air shots towards the goal (6-36). The goalkeeper should catch each shot using the correct technique.

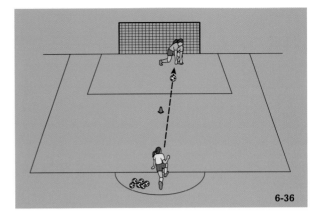

6-36

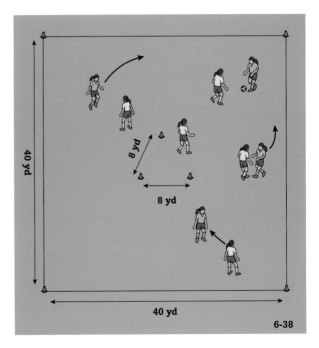

6-37

GOALKEEPING *(Handling—Ground and Air Shots)*

ORGANIZATION Goalkeeper, one player with a number of soccer balls, one cone. The goalkeeper stands in the goal on the goal line. The player stands 10 yards out from the goal with a ball. The goalkeeper sprints forward and touches the cone at the edge of the six-yard box (6-37). As the goalkeeper retreats backwards, the player throws the soccer ball high overhead for the goalkeeper to deflect or catch. Repeat the exercise.

GOALKEEPING *(Handling, Including Footwork)*

FIELD SIZE 40 yds x 40 yds.

ORGANIZATION Four-on-four plus a goalkeeper, one soccer ball, seven cones. The cones are set out as goals in a triangular pattern eight yards apart in the middle of the grid. A four-on-four confrontation is played where both teams can score through any of the three goals (6-38). The goalkeeper must scurry between all goals and attempt to keep both teams from scoring. If a save is made, the goalkeeper serves the ball back anywhere within the grid area.

6-38

GOALKEEPING *(Shot Stopping)*

ORGANIZATION Goalkeeper, one player with a number of soccer balls. The goalkeeper stands in the middle of the goal. The player stands on the six-yard line with the soccer balls and rolls a ball along the ground to the side, forcing the goalkeeper to make a low, diving save (6-39). The player follows by playing another ball high to the opposite side, making the goalkeeper dive high to save it. Have players repeat this exercise ten times, remembering to alternate the serving passes high and low and from side to side.

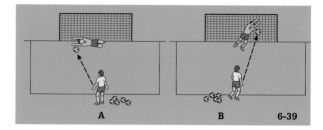

GOALKEEPING *(Shot Stopping)*

ORGANIZATION Goalkeeper, one player with a number of soccer balls, eight cones. The goalkeeper stands in the middle of the goal. The player stands 10 to 12 yards from the goal with the soccer balls. The cones are placed across the six-yard line (6-40). The player plays the ball towards the goalkeeper while attempting to hit one of the cones. The cone deflects the ball and forces the goalkeeper to dive to make the save.

GOALKEEPING *(Shot Stopping & Supporting the Defense)*

FIELD SIZE 30 yds x 20 yds.

ORGANIZATION Two-on-two plus two goalkeepers. Play two-on-two with emphasis on shot stopping, communication, and support of teammates (6-41).

GOALKEEPING (Distribution)

FIELD SIZE Half of the field.

ORGANIZATION Goalkeeper, two players with a number of soccer balls. Position the goalkeeper in the goal area. Two players are positioned one on each side of the penalty area. They take turns at crossing the ball to the goalkeeper, who catches it and throws it out to the player on the opposite side of the penalty area (6-42). The player receiving the ball is free to move anywhere down the side of the field. This will encourage the goalkeeper to look and switch play.

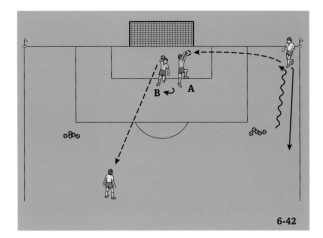

6-42

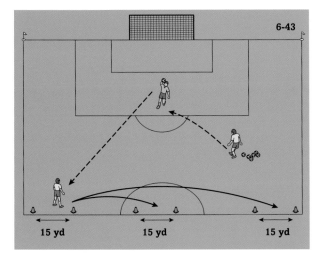

6-43

GOALKEEPING (Distribution)

FIELD SIZE Half of the field.

ORGANIZATION Goalkeeper, two players with a number of soccer balls, six cones. The cones are set up 15 yards apart along the center line. The goalkeeper receives a ball from the serving player (6-43). The goalkeeper then distributes (kicks or throws) it to the other player, who calls and is free to move into any one of the three target areas. This will encourage the goalkeeper to look before distributing the ball.

15 yd   15 yd   15 yd

GOALKEEPING (Distribution)

FIELD SIZE Half of the field

ORGANIZATION Goalkeeper, three players with a number of soccer balls. The players on each side of the penalty box take turns at crossing the ball into the penalty area for the goalkeeper to collect (6-44). The goalkeeper can distribute it back to either of the serving players or to the third player positioned in the center of the field. As the goalkeeper becomes more competent, the coach should designate which player the goalkeeper should distribute to. This will encourage the goalkeeper in decision-making and quick distribution.

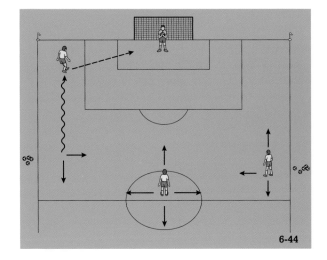

6-44

GOALKEEPING
(Narrowing the Angle)

ORGANIZATION Goalkeeper, one player with ten soccer balls. The player runs forward and shoots each ball in turn from alternate ends of the row (6-45). Before each shot, the goalkeeper must narrow the angle and attempt to save, then readjust for the next shot.

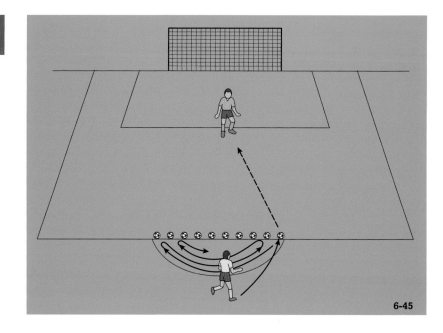

6-45

GOALKEEPING (Narrowing the Angle)

FIELD SIZE 44 yds x 36 yds.

ORGANIZATION Twelve players and two goalkeepers with a number of soccer balls. Practice takes place in a double-size penalty area with full-size goals. To start the practice, one of the goalkeepers rolls a ball out to a player on the right side (6-46). The receiving player is chased by another player coming from the opposite side of the goal. The goalkeeper at the far end advances and attempts to narrow the angle and make the save. The receiving goalkeeper should now roll the ball to the right, repeating the exercise. Duplicate this exercise ten times, then change the service to the left.

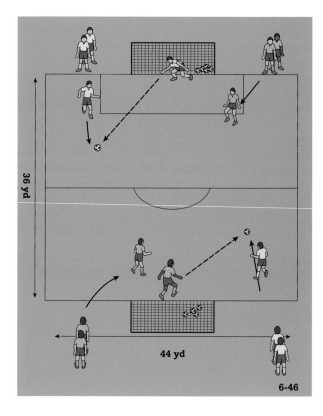

36 yd

44 yd

6-46

FIELD SIZE 40 yds x full field width.

ORGANIZATION Four-on-two, plus a goalkeeper and one other player with a number of soccer balls. The serving player passes the ball to any one of the four attacking players. With no offside law and the advantage in numbers, the attacking players should have many opportunities to dribble past or shoot at the goalkeeper (6-47). Once the attackers have broken clear of the defenders, the goalkeeper can practice the skill of narrowing the angle. Encourage the goalkeeper to communicate with the defenders.

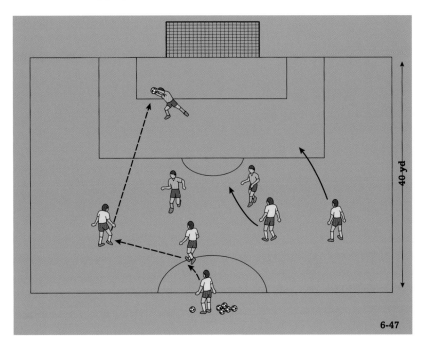

6-47

FIELD SIZE Half of the field.

ORGANIZATION Two players; two goalkeepers, each with a number of soccer balls. One goalkeeper throws a ball to the player on the right, who controls and pushes it forward before crossing it to the other goalkeeper (6-48). The receiving goalkeeper collects it and repeats the exercise. Have player repeat 10 times to the right, then switch to the left to enable the goalkeepers to practice collecting crosses from each side.

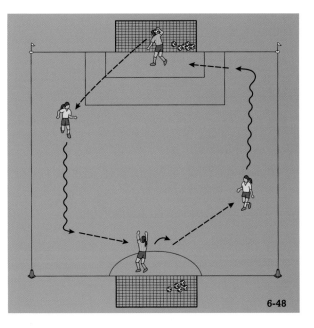

6-48

FIELD SIZE Half of the field.

ORGANIZATION Three players and one defender, plus a goalkeeper and a number of balls. The serving player passes the ball out to one of the players on the wing. The wing player plays it forward before crossing it into the goal area (6-49). Player repeat the exercise, passing the ball at varying heights and angles, with the goalkeeper deciding which one should clear the cross.

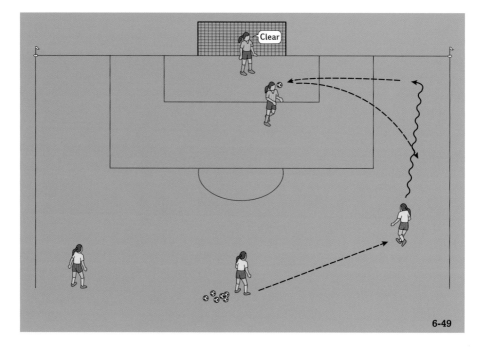

6-49

FIELD SIZE Half of the field.

ORGANIZATION 10 players; two goalkeepers, each with a number of soccer balls. One of the goalkeepers throws a ball out to either of the wide players, who play it forward before crossing it towards two attacking players in the goal area (6-50). The crosses should be varied between the near and far posts, encouraging the goalkeeper to make decisions and communicate with the defenders. The practice is then repeated from the opposite end.

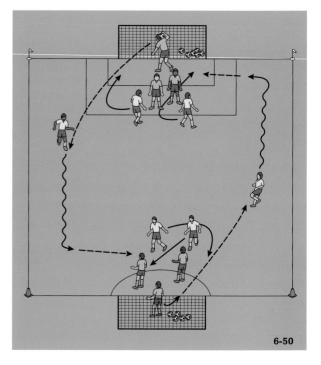

6-50

Team Games

FIELD SIZE Half of the field.

ORGANIZATION 10 players plus two goalkeepers, one soccer ball, 16 cones, one portable goal. Set out the half-field with the portable goal and smaller, cone-indicated goals at the corners on the goal line at each end. Play five-on-five with the exception of corner kicks. Teams get one point for scoring on the goalkeeper and half a point for scoring on the small cone goals (6-51). Always play to a half-point total—e.g., 5½, 6½—to encourage scoring on the small goals.

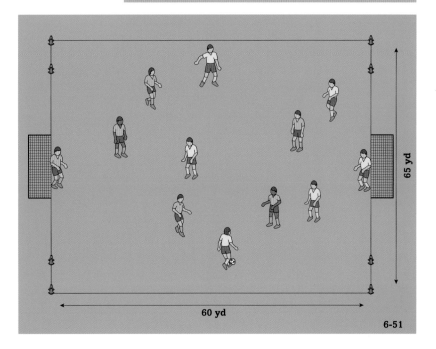

Coaching Points
- Spreading the opposition.
- Attacking wide down the wings.
- Switching the point of attack.

65 yd

60 yd

6-51

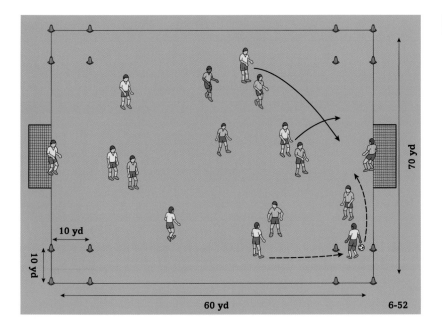

70 yd

10 yd

10 yd

60 yd

6-52

TEAM GAMES

FIELD SIZE Half of the field.

ORGANIZATION Equal teams plus goalkeepers, one soccer ball, 16 cones, one portable goal. Set out the field with the portable goal and 10-yard by 10-yard cone grids at the goal line in each corner. Playing normal soccer, each team attempts to free a player into one of the grids (6-52). Once in this grid area, the player should deliver a cross.

FIELD SIZE 60 yds x 40 yds.

ORGANIZATION Team players numbered one to six, four players without numbers, two goalkeepers, one soccer ball, four cones, one portable goal. Play six-on-four. Once the numbered players have possession of the ball, they must pass it in numerical order (6-53). If the ball is lost, when it is regained, passing is recommended in numerical order from the player that has possession. When the players without numbers have possession of the ball, they should pass it freely.

PROGRESSION Build up to six-on-five and six-on-six.

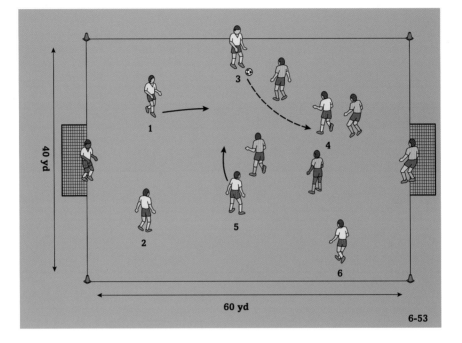

6-53

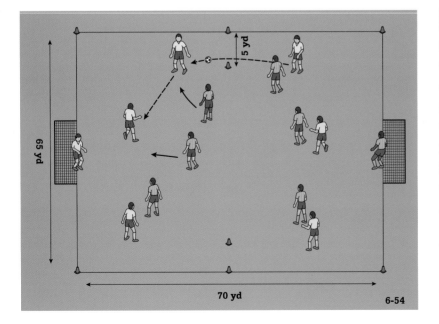

6-54

FIELD SIZE 70 yds x 65 yds.

ORGANIZATION Teams with an equal number of players plus goalkeepers, one soccer ball, eight cones. Once a team wins possession of the ball, it must be played through one of the two cone gates before a goal can be scored (6-54). The ball can be thrown in with a correct throw-in, dribbled, or passed through either of the gates from either side.

FIELD SIZE 45 yds x 15 yds.

ORGANIZATION Six players, one soccer ball, 12 cones. Set up three 10-yard by 10-yard grids in a triangle that is 15 yards by 45 yards. Play three-on-one in one grid, with a single player in the other two grids (6-55). The three players complete a series of passes, then chip the ball to a player in one of the other two grids. The three players sprint to that grid; the last player to arrive becomes the defender, and the exercise is repeated. To keep the runners from cheating, the defender performs 20 push-ups after the attackers leave the grid.

PROGRESSION Change the point of attack; play four-on-two and increase up to five grids.

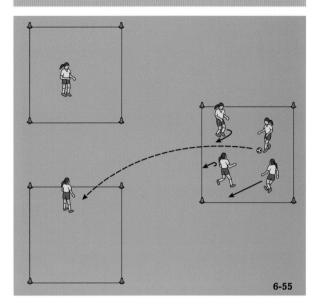

6-55

TEAM GAMES

FIELD SIZE Half of the field.

ORGANIZATION 12 players plus two goalkeepers, one soccer ball. The goalkeepers are the target and are restricted, one to the six-yard box and the other to half of the center circle (6-56). The teams attempt to play the ball to a target. If the ball is delivered from a wide position, a lofted pass must be used. If the ball is delivered from a central position, a ground shot must be used. As soon as a team reaches the target, the ball is distributed back to that same team, which then attacks in the opposite direction.

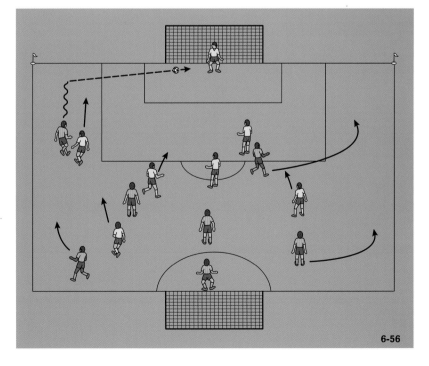

6-56

About the Authors

ROBERT "BUTCH" LAUFFER is a widely recognized soccer mentor, guiding his West Texas A&M University teams through numerous winning seasons, with more than 15 seasons as head men's coach and more than 10 as head women's coach.

Mr. Lauffer is certified with the United States Soccer Federation (USSF) Class "A" license as well as the English Football Association's preparatory coaching license. He is recognized by the Irish Football Association with a Grade 1 coaching license. He has also earned his United European Football Association (UEFA) Class "A" License from the Wales Football Association and earned a UEFA pro license through the Scottish Football Association.

Among his many soccer honors, he was named NCAA Midwest Region Coach of the Year in 2001 and received Lone Star Conference Men's Coach of the Year award in 1999 and 2000. He was also chosen as the Women's LSC Coach of the Year in 1996 and 2001.

He has hosted more than ten Annual International Soccer Coaches' Clinics in Dallas, Texas. During the 1994 World Cup, he assisted FIFA with the technical reports at the Dallas venue. He is a USSF National Staff Coach. As part of this program, he has taught the "A," "B," and "C" level coaches through coaching clinics on further developing their coaching skills. He is also director of soccer for the Amarillo Drifters Soccer Association.

He earned both his bachelor's degree in kinesiology and his master's degree from Texas Christian University in Fort Worth while working as a graduate assistant in their soccer program. In his playing days, he competed for the Texas Longhorn Soccer Club, a team with which he logged over 100 international matches. He is the author of *Coaching Soccer, Soccer Coach's Guide to Practices, Drills & Skill Training* (with Sandy Davie), and *Women's Soccer: Techniques, Tactics & Teamwork* (with April Kater).

Mr. Lauffer was born in Washington, D.C., moved to Dallas at age seven, and has played or coached soccer ever since. He lives in Amarillo with his wife Kim and their two children, Kendall and Kyle.

ALEXANDER "SANDY" DAVIE is a fully qualified USSF Licensed Coach. He also holds coaching accreditations from the New Zealand Soccer Association as well as the Irish Football Association.

As a former State Staff Coach with the Florida Youth Soccer Association, his most recent coaching achievements include three years at the helm of the New Zealand Women's National Team and three years as Goalkeeper Coach to the New Zealand Men's National Team.

Sandy's coaching abilities stem from a professional playing career, which began when Scottish Premier League Team Dundee United signed him at age fifteen as their goalkeeper.

He represented Scotland at Youth and Under 23 levels, and during his nine years with Dundee United played over 200 games for them, including the club's first ever Scottish Cup Final appearance against Glasgow Celtic at Hampden Park. Sandy has also played in European Cup competition against Barcelona and Atletico Bilbao of Spain, as well as the Italian giants Juventus.

During his distinguished playing career, Sandy also spent two years with Luton Town in the English First Division, playing over 100 games for them, before transferring to Southampton of the English Premier League.

Index